New and Revised Edition.

THE HEAVENLY RECOGNITION;

OR,

AN EARNEST AND SCRIPTURAL DISCUSSION

OF THE QUESTION,

WILL WE KNOW OUR FRIENDS IN HEAVEN?

BY

REV. H. HARBAUGH, A.M.

AUTHOR OF "HEAVEN; OR, THE SAINTED DEAD."

She goeth unto the grave to weep there.
JOHN xi. 31.

Fifteenth Edition.

PHILADELPHIA:
LINDSAY & BLAKISTON.
1861.

STEREOTYPED BY J. FAGAN. PRINTED BY C. SHERMAN.

TO

THE REV. DAVID HARBAUGH,

MY YOUNGEST BROTHER,

UNDER WHOSE ENCOURAGING INQUIRIES

THESE PAGES HAVE,

FOR THREE YEARS,

BEEN PROGRESSING TOWARD THEIR PRESENT

COMPLETION:

AND

TO WHOM I FEEL JOINED

FOREVER

IN KINDRED AND IN CHRIST,

This Volume,

IN FIRM FAITH OF THE

HEAVENLY RECOGNITION,

IS AFFECTIONATELY

DEDICATED.

PREFACE

TO

THE REVISED EDITION.

THE ninth edition of the "HEAVENLY RECOGNITION" being called for, we have, with great care, given the work a thorough revision, and now again send it forth to the public, free from a few verbal and typographical errors which occurred in the former editions.

We humbly acknowledge God's goodness in giving it so much favor with Christians of all denominations, in our native land as well as in England; and also for the assurance we have received from Christian friends that the work has been a source of light and consolation to many bereaved hearts.

LANCASTER, September, 1855.

PREFACE.

Our friends in Heaven—shall we see and know them again? This is my theme. I have written this book because I love the subject of which it treats. It was, therefore, not a toil, but a pleasure. It was in my heart before it was in my mind; and it grew up there like a flower, living and fragrant, to my own soul. If life, warmth, and tenderness do not now glow upon its leaves, it is because the mind has spoiled the image in transferring the impression. What a pity, we are sometimes tempted to say, that it is so hard to make a picture for others of what we ourselves see and feel! I have done as well as I could.

Three years ago, the Author published a work entitled: "Heaven; or, An Earnest and Scriptural Inquiry into the Abode of the Sainted Dead." While writing that book, the thought of writing this gradually waked up in my mind: hence, at the close of that book occurs the following passage: "Here I lay down my pen, but here do I not end my meditations on the heavenly land. My thoughts, and feelings, and hopes, crowd onward still." That may be taken as a promise or prophecy of what is here fulfilled. Here, accordingly, we offer the fruits of three years' farther meditation on the heavenly world. We feel the more encouragement in offering this additional contribution to this department of pious inquiry, because it is one of those peaceful themes which, even in the present distracted and divided state of the church, is not likely to excite any sectional jealousies. In the hope of another and a better life, we are all one.

The Author believes that human nature generally, and particularly in this age, is too prone to disjoin the material and spiritual, the finite and infinite, the temporal and eternal, and, consequently, also the kingdom on earth and the kingdom in heaven. God, in the Incarnation of his Son, has for ever united these, and brought them into living and loving sympathy with each other. Time and space are annihilated in "Jesus Christ, the same yesterday, and to-day, and for ever." In Him we are raised above the ruins of the Past — above the changes of the Present — and above the fears of the Future. In proportion as we rise, by faith in Him, above all fragmentary and sectional ideas into communion with the general, the catholic, the infinite, and the absolute—in that proportion will we escape the downward tendencies towards the sordid regions of sense, and the more refined but chilling abstractions of Rationalism, both in its spiritualistic and materialistic extremes. God has made the heavens above us higher, broader, deeper, and more magnificent than the earth, that we might be overawed by them; and he has made them more bright and beautiful than the earth, that they might allure us. Morally, as well as physically, God has hung the earth fast to the heavens, and controls it by a law of gravitation whose centre is *there*; and hereby He would shadow forth to us the truth, that our spirits, in all their affections, should hinge and turn upon the high, the infinite, the heavenly. Our proper position therefore is, to stand like the high-priest before the altar, and, in devout reverence and worship, to stretch forth our hands towards the heavens, while our hearts also rise thitherward in humble but earnest hope and love. We must embrace the infinite and heavenly, in all its forms, if we would be devout.

We, therefore, firmly believe that our hearts will become better by being filled with heavenly thoughts. This can be done by sitting together in heavenly places in Christ Jesus, and meditating upon the eternal inheritance which He has in reserve for us. The reader will discover how much Christ is made the centre and substance of this book; and how the hope of our eternal union with our sainted friends is ultimately resolved into our union with Him. This is a feature in this doctrine of future recognition—and the most important one—which we have not been able to discover in all that we have found written on this subject, in any degree of prominence. We believe that this is the real basis of the doctrine, which serves to make all other arguments in its favor consistent and living. To this feature, and to the historical manner in which we have treated the subject, we respectfully invite the reader's special attention, as being, in our estimation, of the greatest importance.

We have carefully studied all we could find on this interesting subject, and acknowledge ourselves more or less indebted to those from whom we occasionally quote, and whose names are generally referred to, or placed in the margin. We have aimed at making this a full discussion of the subject; and have therefore pursued it, so far as we could find any light to lead us, into all its details. This has enlarged the book, but it will hardly be considered a fault. We have not consciously admitted any thing irrelevant.

It will be seen, we hope, on every page that we have not followed the subject as one merely of vain curiosity, but with a sincere desire also that it might produce its practical fruits. We have been anxious that it should not only afford consolation, but also make the heart better. We have endeavored to keep prominently before the mind of the reader the solemn fact that the heavenly society of which this book treats it *may* never be *his* happiness to enjoy, — that the only ground upon which he can safely rest his hope of reunion in heaven with his sainted friends is his own personal union on earth with Him "of whom the whole family in heaven and earth is named."

Standing in the deepest reverence of soul before the solemn mysteries of that holy world into which this book presumes to cast an humble look, and in the name of our adorable Saviour, I lay this offering at His sacred feet. May He pardon what is wrong, and bless what is good, to the consolation of the saints, and to the advancement of His own great Kingdom of Eternal Love.

LANCASTER, Sept. 8, 1851.

CONTENTS.

CHAPTER I.

THE SAINTED DEAD.

Introductory reflections ....Page 17

CHAPTER II.

THE HEAVENLY RECOGNITION AMONG PAGANS.

Pagan ideas of a future life. The earnest expectation of the creature. Why this chapter is introduced. The idea of future recognition in Homer's poems. The ideas of Socrates. Beautiful quotation. The heathen commit suicide in sorrow that they may meet their friends sooner in the future life. Widows burning themselves on the funeral pyres of their husbands. Sacrificing human beings as attendants at the death of kings and chiefs. Sending messages with the dead — the Gymnosophists. The idea of future recognition among Roman philosophers. Cicero—extract. Virgil. Modern pagans. Extract from Dr. Leland. The Indians of America. Slaves from Africa. Sighings and sorrowings. Comforts. Friendships. Skeptics. Live and love. No tears for the dead.......... 24

CHAPTER III.

THE HEAVENLY RECOGNITION A UNIVERSAL BELIEF, HOPE, AND DESIRE.

This faith is universal. So is the desire. All universal ideas are true. This is proved from the idea of the existence of a God — the soul's immortality — sacrifice and atonement. Fragments prove a whole. Reason never reaches the universal. Humanity is no lie. The idea of future recognition spontaneous. Farther deductions and proofs from its universality. I. This idea grows with Christianity. II. It grows in each heart with grace. III. It is more firmly held by saints than by sinners. IV. It is most active in the deepest sorrow. Universal desire is also a proof of its truth in the same way. Practical observations. The human race a brotherhood. The world is not all fragments. The kingdom of the dead a catholic kingdom. Human tears promote fellowship. Love for the dead. Communion with them 46

CHAPTER IV.

THE HEAVENLY RECOGNITION IN THE LIGHT OF REASON.

The dead before the resurrection. No separate discussion necessary. Why? Spiritual peculiarities by which recognition can take place. Spirits not human do know each other. The scriptures make no difference. Will recognition take place *on sight*, or *gradually?* Exhibitions of both. Why is this doctrine reasonable. I. The same means which will enable us to identify ourselves will also enable us to recognize our friends. II. Memory will continue in the future life. III. The social law lies deeply and radically imbedded in our nature. IV. Some interruptions by death, which seem, in the nature of things, to require completion in a future life. V. The final Judgment involves details which show that recognition is reasonable and natural. VI. Our knowledge, in the future life, will be enlarged in general and in particular. VII. The interest which heavenly beings take in the affairs of saints on earth induces us to believe the idea of future recognition reasonable. A pleasant conclusion 66

CHAPTER V.

THE HEAVENLY RECOGNITION AMONG THE JEWS.

The Jewish twilight. Progress in this doctrine. The Jews knew of a future life. They believed in future recognition. Proofs. I. The care and affection with which they disposed of the bodies of their dead points to the hope and belief in future reunion. II. Their strong desire to be buried with their kindred. III. The manner in which they spake of their dead, as "gathered to their people." IV. This doctrine is seen in some examples of pure and disinterested friendship. V. This doctrine is seen in the conduct of David at the death of his child, and the way he consoled himself. VI. This doctrine appears also in later prophets. This faith among the Jews was implicit. 85

CHAPTER VI.

THE HEAVENLY RECOGNITION IN THE TEACHINGS OF CHRIST.

The object of Christ's mission into the world. He spake incidentally of heaven. The doctrine of heavenly recognition in hints and allusions. Proofs. I. This doctrine is involved in the nature of that kingdom which Christ established on earth, and which is to continue in heaven. II. We see this doctrine in what Christ says of heaven as the home of the saints. III. We find this doctrine in the Saviour's representations of the final Judgment. IV. This doctrine appears in several passages of the Saviour's teachings. We first feel it true, and then know it. Conclusion. Poetry by Bp. Mant 116

CHAPTER VII.

THE HEAVENLY RECOGNITION AMONG THE APOSTLES.

The Apostles' ideas of another life — of the kingdom of Christ — of our union with each other in this kingdom — of the identity of the Church on earth and in heaven. Hints and allusions. They expected to present their converts in the day of Christ's coming. The pastor's joy, hope, and crown in heaven. Those asleep in Jesus—true consolation in regard to them. A look into heaven from Patmos, and sights which were seen. Charity never faileth. Holy love, and mere passion. A beautiful poem by Southey. Light from a happy land 142

CHAPTER VIII.

THE HEAVENLY RECOGNITION AMONG THE CHRISTIAN FATHERS.

Why we desire to know their sentiments. The affection they showed towards their pious dead. They visit the place where they are buried. Their desire for martyrdom. Their horror at the Roman practice of burning the bodies of the dead. The affecting burial of Cyprian by his flock. They associated the remembrance of the dead with their religious services. They buried them around the church. They celebrated the anniversary of their death upon the graveyards. Partook of the communion in token of an unbroken union with them. Quotation from Neander. Cyprian consoling his flock. Drawing near to the dead in love. Heavenly attractions — an extract. St. Ambrose. Venerable and anointed ideas.... 159

CHAPTER IX.

THE HEAVENLY RECOGNITION AMONG THEOLOGIANS.

The value of this kind of testimony. No new or strange idea. Its catholicity. A clear and fresh stream among fragments.. 170

SECTION I.—ARGUMENTATIVE EXTRACTS.

Dr. Martin Luther. Melancthon. Cruciger. Olevianus. Scaliger. Calvin. Thomas Bacon. Arch. Wm. Paley. Rev. Charles Drelincourt. Rev. Dr. Edwards. Rev. Dr. George Christian Knapp. Rev. John Dick, D. D. Rev. Bp. George Burgess. Rev. William Jay. Rev. J. W. Nevin, D. D.. 172

SECTION II.—ALLUSIONS TO THIS IDEA, TAKING IT FOR GRANTED.

Rev. Dr. John Tillotston. Rev. Richard Baxter. Bishop Hall. Dr. Doddridge. Melvill. Rev. Dr. J. F. Berg... 183

SECTION III.—CONSOLATORY EXTRACTS.

Ulrich Zwinglius. Bunyan. Rev. William Dodd, D. D. George Herbert. Dr. P. Doddridge. Lavel. Dr. Thomas Chalmers. Rev. John Newton. Fenelon. Rev. John James, D. D. Rev. Thomas Smyth, D. D. Rev. S. S. Schmucker, D. D. 187

CHAPTER X.

THE HEAVENLY RECOGNITION AMONG THE POETS.

Orpheus. The power of music and poetry. A still sweeter charmer. The true end of poetry.................... 195

Section I.—argumentative poetry.

Recognition in Heaven. Heavenly Recognition. The Drawings of the Dead. The Indian Mother. Love. Knowledge of each other in Heaven. Not lost, but gone before 197

Section II.—incidental allusions.

How easily the heart slides into this idea. How extensively it is taken for granted. Something for mothers alone. The dead will receive us into heaven. The strongest desire of bereaved hearts. The love of sisters. Proverbial poetry. The heavenly meeting. A secret which all cannot possess. An increasing treasure. A treasure removed, but not lost. A Mother's Lament. Departed friends. Visions by starlight. Heber's portrait. A mother's picture in the parlor. The Dying Child 203

Section III.—consolatory poetry.

The vein which poets follow. The idea on which they end. Leaving ninety and nine, and seeking one that is lost. Sorrow makes us dull. The poet a confidential friend. They speak in us. Reunion above. Rev. Charles Wesley. Sorrow with hope. The babe that only sleeps. A thought for an unconverted person. My Boy. Not lost, but gone before. Treasures in the arms of Christ. Dreams of Heaven. The Burial of an Emigrant's Child. Weep not for her. Something for social singing circles. Reunion above. A beautiful vision through a tear. Kiss the hand that wounds you. Unwritten poetry. Sarah B. Judson—a "green islet" in the ocean, and a grave on it. A ray in deep darkness 212

CHAPTER XI.

OBJECTIONS TO THE DOCTRINE OF HEAVENLY RECOGNITION.

Introductory remarks 231
OBJ. I.—The great change which will take place in death.. 233
OBJ. II.—If it were true, it would be more clearly revealed. 239
OBJ. III.—The heavenly life will be much higher than this. 241
OBJ. IV.—It will introduce partiality into heaven 242
OBJ. V.—The love of Christ will occupy us entirely....... 244
OBJ. VI.—Christ's answer to the Sadducees 246

CHAPTER XII.

ANOTHER OBJECTION TO THE DOCTRINE OF HEAVENLY RECOGNITION.

THE KNOWLEDGE OF OUR LOST FRIENDS WOULD GIVE US PAIN.

This objection appeals more to the feeling than to the judgment. It can be satisfactorily answered. Various considerations. I. In death all ties that are not sanctified by the life and power of grace must be dropped and left behind. II. Those that are lost will gradually fade from our remembrance. III. There may be room for some uncertainty as to whether they are lost or not. IV. We have positive evidence that a knowledge of beings lost, who were once objects of affection, is not incompatible with heavenly felicity. The case of Christ—of angels. V. Our will will be entirely conformed to God's will. Instances as illustrations. Poetry...................... 253

CHAPTER XIII.

THE DOCTRINE OF HEAVENLY RECOGNITION IN ITS PRACTICAL EFFECTS.

"What good?" The tendency of error — of truth. The Saviour's rule. The belief in this doctrine exerts a good influence. I. It elevates, strengthens, and purifies all our earthly affections. II. It will induce us to form only pious friendships. III. It will bring us strongly under the power of heavenly realities and attractions. IV. It presents a strong and touching motive to piety. V. It is consoling to the pious under bereavements. The end ... 273

THE

HEAVENLY RECOGNITION.

CHAPTER I.

The Sainted Dead.

My mother! when I learned that thou wast dead,
Say, wast thou conscious of the tears I shed?
Hover'd thy spirit o'er thy sorrowing son,
Wretch even then, life's journey just begun!
Perhaps thou gav'st me, though unfelt, a kiss;
Perhaps a tear, if souls can weep in bliss—
Ah, that maternal smile! it answers—yes!
I heard the bell toll'd on the burial day,
I saw the hearse that bore thee slow away,
And, turning from my nurs'ry window, drew
A long, long sigh, and wept a last adieu!
But was it such?—It was.—Where thou art gone,
Adieus and farewells are a sound unknown.
May I but meet thee on that peaceful shore,
The parting word shall pass my lips no more!

COWPER.

THE Sainted Dead! they are our treasures! Like the inheritance upon which they have entered, they are incorruptible, undefiled, and they fade not away, but are reserved in Heaven.

Ho! ye that would be rich—ye that seek for treasures—seek them not on earth. Earth yields only that which is mortal and perishable. That which dies seeks the earth, not that which lives. "Earth to earth, ashes to ashes, dust to dust." This our fathers have repeated, and this they have experienced. They die quickly, the flowers of earth. It rusts soon, the gold of earth. They fade surely, the gems of earth. They must perish, the foundations of earth — if not before, in the flames of the last fire. Ho! ye that seek for treasures: they are our treasures — living treasures — the Sainted Dead.

Let us look upward. That is the destiny of spirits. It is the earth which whirls and moves; the heavens stand permanent and sure. While the earth grows hoary with age, while empires fall and nations die, while the habitations of the dead are becoming more than habitations of the living, while all things around us change and fade, the heavens still look down serene as of old upon this changing and restless earth. The stars which wink to us a loving "upward" — how changeless! They are the same which Abraham and Job saw, and which, ages ago,

> "Gladdened, on their mountain tops, the hearts
> Of the Chaldean shepherds, till they poured
> Themselves in orisons."

So calm, changeless, cheering, and loving, are the saints in light. Not like the false, fading glare of earthly treasures, is their pure and imperishable radiance; for they "shine as the brightness of the firmament, and as the stars for ever and ever." They are our treasures — changeless and shining treasures — the Sainted Dead.

Let us look up hopefully. "Not lost, but gone before." Lost only like the stars of morning that have faded into the light of a brighter heaven. Lost to earth, but not to us. When the earth is dark, then the heavens are bright. When objects around us become indistinct and invisible in the shades of night, then objects above us are more clearly seen. So is the night of sorrow and mourning; it settles down upon us like a lonely twilight at the grave of our friends; but then already they shine on high. While we weep, they sing! While they are with us upon earth, they lie upon our hearts refreshingly, like the dew upon flowers; when they disappear, it is by a power from above that has drawn them upward, and, though lost on the earth, they still float in the skies. Like the dew that is absorbed from the flowers, they will not return to us; but, like the flowers themselves, we will die, yet only to bloom again in the Eden above. Then those whom the heavens have absorbed, and removed from us, by the sweet attraction of their love, made holier and lovelier in light, will draw toward us again by a holy affinity, and rest on our hearts as before. They are our treasures—loving treasures—the Sainted Dead.

Let us look up joyfully. Love is eternal. When the light and smiles of earthly love seem to perish in the grave, then it is night on earth and gloomy. "The setting of a great hope is like the setting of the sun. The brightness of our life is gone. Shadows of evening fall around us, and the world seems but a dim reflection—itself a broader shadow. We look forward into the coming lonely night. The soul withdraws into itself. Then the stars arise, and the night is holy!" All is yet not dark. Heaven kindles anew, across the sea of space, beacons of hope and promise. Though the flowers of love die in our hearts, they lose not their fragrance. The looks, the forms, the voices, the smiles of the dead are still with us. We feel their mysterious nearness. The remembrance of their kindness and love still teaches us to love them.

> Like the vase in which roses have once been distilled—
> You may break, you may ruin the vase if you will;
> But the scent of the roses will hang round it still!

Their names are still to us "like ointment poured forth," the odor of which comes to us richest in our loneliest hours. Their image, lovely as the purest thoughts we can form of them, floats before our waking visions, and smiles upon us in the dreams of the night. Being themselves holy, the light of our love falling upon them becomes holy too. The heart gradually becomes like that which it loves. Purer than we are, our affections are purified by the power of their attractions, as the sides of all objects grow bright that are turned towards the sun. These are our treasures—holy treasures—the Sainted Dead.

Let us look up longingly. Where our treasures are, there let our hearts be also. The heart of the miser is with his gold. The eye of the merchant follows his freighted vessel till it disappears in the dim, distant blue; then looks often into the vacant air that hangs over the broad sea, for its return, till he sees at last its hopeful pennants streaming; and as it draws nearer, his heart grows fuller of grateful wonderment and hope. Now this they do for perishable gain. Let us do the same, yea more, for that which perishes not. If earthly treasures draw the heart so strongly, ought not heavenly treasures more? Yea, but our hearts are so gross and grovelling, and feel so little the sweet attraction of the infinite and the pure. Let us long after them more ardently, our treasures — attractive treasures — the Sainted Dead.

Let us look up lovingly. Love is stronger than all ills, and will crowd itself even through death. Love seeks and finds its object — dies, and yet dies not, in the pursuit. Under its guidance, we shall find the objects of our affections; for it knows the homeward way. Come, ye living! let us sit together under the moaning but ever-green cypress, and commune with the departed. Let us drive from our hearts Cæsar's money-changers, and escape for a moment from the world's benumbing rattle. Let us draw softly down into the quiet border-land along the valley of the shadow of death. We will listen intently. The softest notes that float to our ears across the almost breathless solitude, shall tell us hopeful tales of a better land, and of those who dwell in it. We will cry earnestly into the hollow silence which so holds the lip of death's Lethean Jordan, as to allow it scarce a whisper of sorrow or joy. The earnestness of our voice will bring back tidings to the ear of faith. We will seek them, our treasures — eternal treasures — the Sainted Dead.

Will we see them again?—know them again?—love

them again?—the Sainted Dead. This would we know? We will institute, humbly but earnestly, our questionings.

As "the deepest lore is the most universal," we will pass along the cool sequestered vale of common life, and listen to the deep longings and hopes of those who live and love

"In the low huts of them that toil and groan."

We will ask the mysterious prophetic sighings that come to us out of the Pagan gloom. We will seek for dawnings of hope in the Jewish twilight. We will look for clearer light in the Gospel dawn—He who brought immortality to light will teach us. We will draw nigh to the Apostles when they speak words of comfort to bereaved hearts—some fragments that prove the existence of a loaf shall be ours. The early Christians, whose hearts were still warm from the words of inspired lips, shall make us wise by holy tradition. The wise of after ages, whose minds were clearest because their hearts were purest, shall utter to us right things on this interesting subject. We will sit at the feet of the poets, who are "the interpreters of the human heart—the expounders of its mysteries," and who have an utterance given them that is denied to others; they will not send us empty away.

In all these researches, we cannot fail to gather some rays of sacred wisdom, to shine away the sorrow of bereaved hearts, and much of the gloom of death. Voices, though feeble, and unheard by the dull ear of worldlings, yet comforting as sweet songs of promise, shall answer to our questionings. They will whisper soothingly to us: You shall find them—know them—love them—your fadeless treasures—the Sainted Dead.

Is your heart sad? Do your lips tremble? Are your eyes wet? Then read on in the next chapter, "Blessed are they that mourn: for they shall be comforted."

CHAPTER II.

The Heavenly Recognition among Pagans.

Who would not part with a great deal to purchase a meeting with Orpheus, Hesiod, Homer? If it be true that this is to be the consequence of death, I would even be glad to die often. What pleasure will it give to live with Palemedes and others, who suffered unjustly, and to compare my fate with theirs! What an inconceivable happiness will it be to converse, in another world, with Sisyphus, Ulysses, &c., especially as those who inhabit that world shall die no more."—*Socrates, Apol. apud Plat.*

The ancient Germans hoped to meet their friends again, beyond death, in a beautiful and peaceful valley.—*Ernst.*

THE knowledge of a future life has always been common among pagan tribes and nations. That they should live after death was believed among them from the earliest time, and has been a cherished doctrine with them in all ages, and in all lands. No one among them, however, professed to have deduced the doctrine of the soul's immortality from his own reasonings; neither did any one ever pretend to have received it by direct revelation from spiritual beings. They always speak of it as a very ancient doctrine, found among those golden glimmerings of sacred tradition which appear among all nations, in the grey twilight of their early history, far back as knowledge extends.

This is not strange. Life is sweet, and it is a pleasing hope to live after death. The knowledge of an eternal life, no doubt, came to them by some stray rays of divine revelation that found their way out from the tents of Israel into the surrounding gloom of pagan darkness. These were eagerly caught, warmly cherished, and long retained, because they served in a great measure to interpret the deep and mysterious wants and longings of their hearts. No one can look into the history, literature, poetry and religion of any pagan nation, at any period of the world, without being moved to pity and sympathy at the plaintive expression of their earnest hopes and fears in reference to another life.

What has now been said of their belief in another life itself, is equally true in reference to their belief in the mutual recognition of each other in that life, and the renewal and perpetuation of their earthly friendships and affections. It is necessary, in a full discussion of this subject, to take notice of this, not so much to ascertain what is positively true—that will be attended to in the proper place—as to ascertain what the heart, when left to its own longings, *desires* to be true. These deep, earnest voices and whispers of the human heart, are always prophetic. This cry of want is to be listened to, in order to find out the remedy needed. What God has provided for the saved, will certainly correspond with the wants of the lost before they are saved. These pagan ideas are voices in the wilderness, like that of John the Baptist, which do not contradict the teachings of Him who is to come, but really and truly proclaim what is to come. The "carnest expectation of the creature" will not be disappointed. It is true, in a deep and comprehensive sense, that "hope maketh not ashamed." Hope presupposes a sense of want; hope is the reaching forth of the heart after that which will satisfy its wants. What these wants by an inward necessity reach after, must and does exist. This sense of want exists for the very reason that thereby their hearts may be urged on to seek that which will satisfy them. In this sense we are "saved by hope." This sense of want teaches us that what will satisfy them exists, though it be out of sight; and hence it is that the object of hope must, in the nature of things, be unseen. "Hope that is seen is not hope; for what a man seeth, why doth he yet hope for? But if we hope for that we see not, then do we with patience wait for it."

We introduce this chapter on the doctrine of future recognition among pagans, not only to exhibit the deep desire they manifested that it might be true, and thus to show that a want exists in the human spirit which calls for it; but also to preserve, through the whole discussion, the unbroken thread of its history. It must be granted, by all who earnestly think, that no doctrine can be correctly and clearly treated, or rightly understood and appreciated, except in the light and connection of its past history. Any event or doctrine suddenly sprung upon us, rather confounds than instructs us. Our intellectual and moral nature always starts with a kind of suspicious surprise at that which is new. Only that which is light and frivolous at once falls in with the latest; the deep and thoughtful regards the past. A doctrine, like a prophet, has not the same honor, at the time when it arises, which it has afterwards; age is necessary to give it the authority of wisdom. We cannot possibly so well know an individual who is suddenly introduced to us in mature age, even though his character be delineated to us, as we do know the same person, if we have known him ourselves in all his acts from childhood. In like manner, we cannot have so correct an idea of a doctrine which is abruptly introduced to us and abstractly discussed, as we will have of the same doctrine when we trace it, from its early and feeble dawnings, through all the phases of its historical evolutions. Ideas, like the fragments of a broken body, may be arranged in their proper and consistent order; but they will have neither life nor beauty unless they have grown together —this requires time—history. We desire, therefore, to exhibit this interesting doctrine in its early dawnings and prophetic glimmerings, as well as in its full and perfect glory.

Homer, the great ancient Grecian poet, who lived and wrote about nine hundred years before Christ,

"The blind old man of Scio's rocky isle,"

as the voice of his age, speaks frequently — sometimes direct, and sometimes incidentally — of the state of the dead. The sentiments he expresses are those of the age in which he lived, as they floated around him in mystic and sacred tradition. He does but define, and utter more clearly than they could have done, what all believed. According to his representations, the shades of the dead retain all the characteristics, dispositions, habits, stations, and peculiarities, which belonged to them before death.* There, in the shadowy land of disembodied spirits, dead heroes meet each other and hold conversations, retaining their earthly distinctive characters. There his hero is

—— Still a master-ghost; the rest he awed;
The rest adored him; towering as he trod;
Still at his side is Nestor's son surveyed,
And loved Patroclus still attends his shade.
Odyssey, Book XXIV., line 25.

In the eleventh book of the Odyssey, Homer represents Ulysses as visiting the shades of the dead. There he meets many whom he knew on earth. There, "wandering through the gloom," he discovered "Elpener's shade," and also that of Tiressias, with both of which he holds conversation; the latter informs him, in prophetic strains, of his coming fortunes. He meets also the shades of ancient heroes and heroines; among them particularly Ajax, "a gloomy shade;" also Patroclus and Achilles, whom he finds in company with each other, having always been friends in life. With Achilles he speaks of the affairs of earth, who, in the course of the conversation, institutes a comparison between life on earth and life in the shades; and wishes to know whether his son, still upon the earth, strives to "emulate his father's godlike deeds."

He meets also his mother! It is an affecting scene! He hastes to embrace her, but she vanishes as a dream from before him—he being still in the flesh—while he exclaims, in true tenderness and affection:

* Vide Odyssey, Book II., line 48, &c.

Fliest thou, loved shade, while I thus fondly mourn!
Turn to my arms, to my embraces turn!
Is it, ye powers that smile at human harms,
Too great a bliss to weep within her arms!

Thus, through the whole of this book, life among the departed is just like life upon earth, as to its social features; it has the same warm and sensible accompaniments as it has here, and looks just as home-like and natural to us. They meet, know, address, love, and hate one another, just as they did upon the earth.

Socrates, who flourished about four hundred years before Christ, had many celebrated disciples, among whom was the great Plato; his sentiments may therefore be fairly taken as the sentiments of his age, and the age immediately succeeding him. In judging of the views of Socrates, and other philosophers of that time, it is necessary to keep in mind, that, as the doctrine of another life itself was not so clearly and fully known as to enable their earnest minds to repose calmly upon it, so it was also with their ideas of the future recognition of friends. It was, with them, like the doctrine of another life itself, a tradition pleasant, ancient, and venerable, which accorded with the wants and wishes of their hearts, rather than a doctrine resting upon a logical basis to satisfy the mind. Hence they speak of it in the varying language of human feeling; at times confidently, and at times with the waverings of painful uncertainty.

In the beginning of the Phædon, Socrates says to those who came to see him in prospect of death, when he was about to place the fatal hemlock to his lips, that it would be wrong in him not to be troubled at the

3 *

idea of dying, "did he not think that he should go to wise and just gods, and to men that had departed this life." "But know assuredly," he adds, "that I hope I am now going to good men, though this I would not take upon me peremptorily to assert."

This dark and trembling uncertainty in the mind of this dying philosopher is caused by a temporary failing of his faith in the ancient tradition, at this trying hour. There is for a moment a rising of his fears above his faith. For this very reason, however, the testimony of this earnest spirit bears more strongly on this subject. It shows that it is not the *mind* of Socrates which speaks its cold logic, but it is his *heart* that deeply utters its hopes and fears. It is not so much his views as his feelings, which he expresses — yea rather, not his feelings, but the feelings of the whole heathen mind, as they had gathered strength more and more from remote and hoary ages, and at length uttered themselves in trembling but earnest prophecy from the heart and lips of dying Socrates. Such a voice from the burdened bosom of pagan wants and woes, has deep significance. Its very tremblings are an evidence of its aged, hoary, and sage-like authority. The pagan heart, pressed thus to the solemn verge of mortal hopes and fears, shall it not feel a want, and have a right to express it, too? Yes; and this want will not be one that is not real, for the satisfaction of which the very constitution of human nature does not rightfully ask, and for which God has not fully provided, if this provision is sought after in the true way. Fallen human nature utters not a single groan for which there is not a remedy. It is fully true that

"Earth hath no sorrow that heaven cannot heal."

The very existence of this sense of want in the pagan heart is, therefore, a true prophecy that Christianity will satisfy it. This "earnest expectation of the creature" points towards a blessed hope, to which all the heirs of life will surely attain — the future finding again of all their sainted friends.

When the heart of Socrates was most humble and tender, and when his own wisdom was most under the powerful influence of simple faith in the ancient tradition, then he spake with more confidence, and in a firmer and more hopeful tone. This is the case in the following passage. Though it commences with a trembling and fearful "if," yet it soon warms up, and rises into the joyful assurance of a calm faith. "If the common expression be true, that death conveys us to those regions which are inhabited by the spirits of departed men, will it not be unspeakably happy to escape from the hands of mere nominal judges, to appear before those who truly deserve the name, such as Minos and Rhadamanthus, and to associate with all who have maintained the cause of truth and rectitude? Is it possible for you to look upon this as an unimportant journey? Is it nothing to converse with Orpheus, and Homer, and Hesiod? Believe me, I would cheerfully suffer many a death on the condition of realizing such a privilege. With what pleasure could I leave the world to hold communion with Palemedes, Ajax, and others, who, like me, have had an unjust sentence pronounced against them? Then would I explore the wisdom of Ulysses, Sisyphus, and that illustrious chief who led out the vast forces of the Grecian army against the city of Troy. Nor should I be condemned to death for indulging, as I have done here, in free inquiry."

Thus spake Socrates to his judges and friends, shortly after he had been sentenced to drink the poisonous hemlock, which ended his mortal career. Though the gloomy "if" troubled him, yet it is plain to see that the hope of meeting the great and good of earth in the future life was stronger than his fears, and shed a soul-cheering light upon his dying hour.

We are told that many of the lower orders among the ancients committed suicide, in the fit of sorrow caused by the death of friends, in order the sooner to be with them again upon immortal shores. Socrates refers to this fact. "Are there not numbers," says he, "who, upon the death of their lovers, wives, and children, have chosen of their own accord to enter Hades, induced by the hope of seeing there those they loved, and of living with them again?"

The custom which has long prevailed, and which still prevails among the Hindoos, and in India generally, of widows burning themselves on the funeral pyre of their beloved husbands, can only be explained on the principle that they expected to follow them into the future life. "She would hasten to the society of him she loves—she would meet him in the spacious halls of Brahma, to spend happier days than were ever realized on earth."

In like manner we must interpret the custom of sacrificing human victims at the death of a chief, which has prevailed among some pagans from ancient times, and is common among the tribes of India. These are expected to attend him, as one they were wont to obey, defend, and honor. This custom, and the intention of it, are hinted at by Homer in his Iliad, Book XXIII., line 211, where Achilles is said to sacrifice four horses, two dogs, and twelve human beings, in connection with the funeral honors of Patroclus, "selected to attend their lord."

Four sprightly coursers, with a deadly groan,
Pour forth their lives, and on the pyre are thrown;
Of nine large dogs, domestic at his board,
Fall two, selected to attend their lord;
When last of all, and horrible to tell,
Sad sacrifice! twelve Trojan captives fell!

This custom plainly points out their belief in the continuation of earthly relations and attachments beyond the grave.

It is said that it was customary among the Indian Gymnosophists, or barefooted philosophers, to send messages to their departed friends with such as made known their intention of committing suicide. Porphyry says of them:—"They endure the term of life with reluctance, as a necessary ministry to nature, and hasten to get their souls at liberty from their bodies; and when they appear to be in health, and have no evil upon them to urge them to it, they freely depart out of this life, telling others beforehand of their intention, who, far from hindering them, account them happy, *and give them commissions to their deceased friends.*"

Dr. Leland, in his excellent work on the Necessity of Divine Revelation, says: "In many parts of the world, where they held a life after this, the notion they had of it seems to have been, that it shall be a life perfectly like the present, with the same bodily wants, the same exercises and employments, and the same enjoyments and pleasures, which they had here. Hence it was that among some nations it was customary for the women, the slaves, the subjects and friends of the deceased, to kill themselves, that in the other world they might serve those whom they loved and respected in this. Such was the practice among the ancient Danes, as Bartholimus informs us in his Danish Antiquities."

These are examples of the strength of human affection, even where it is not under the influence of our holy religion. How lovely is this stability of earthly feeling, and how ardently does it hope to be eternal! Who will say that God has planted in the human heart this principle of disinterested affection, the fruits of which are even in this life so beautiful and pleasant, only to end in death!

We have now found and exhibited this doctrine of future recognition among the philosophers and poets of refined and learned Greece, and also among the less cultivated nations and races in the outer gloom of the pagan world; let us now seek it among the polite and polished Romans.—Cicero, the great Roman orator, who flourished about one hundred years before Christ, has left us his sentiments on this subject in a very tender and touching passage. "For my own part, I feel myself transported with the most ardent impatience to join the society of my two departed friends, your illustrious fathers, whose characters I greatly respected, and whose persons I sincerely loved. Nor is this my earnest desire confined to those excellent persons alone with whom I was formerly connected: I ardently wish to visit also those celebrated worthies, of whose honorable conduct I have heard and read much, or whose virtues I have myself commemorated in some of my writings. To this glorious assembly I am speedily advancing; and I would not be turned back in my journey, even on the assured condition that my youth, like that of Pelias, should be again restored.

"O glorious day! when I shall retire from this low and sordid scene, to associate with the divine assembly of departed spirits; and not with those only whom I have just now mentioned, but with my dear Cato, that best of sons and most valuable of men! It was my sad fate to lay his body on the funeral pile, when by the course of nature I had reason to hope he would have performed the same last office to mine. His soul, however, did not desert me, but still looked back on me in its flight to those happy mansions, to which he was assured I should one day follow him. If I seemed to bear his death with fortitude, it was by no means that I did not most sensibly feel the loss I had sustained: it was because I supported myself with the consoling reflection that we could not long be separated."

With what an affecting simplicity are these words spoken! How wonderfully sweet is their consoling influence; and how are we surprised that they are the product of a pagan mind, and the expression of a pagan heart! How does the gloom of death vanish, even in this pagan mind, before the blessed hope of reunion in a better life!

Virgil, the plaintive bard of Mantua, lived and

wrote about fifty years before Christ. In his Æneid, he makes frequent allusion to the state of the dead. In the sixth book, he represents the Sibyl as conducting Æneas through the shades below. As he passed along among them,

He saw his friends, who, whelm'd beneath the waves,
Their funeral honors claimed, and asked their quiet graves.
The lost Leneaspis in the crowd he knew,
Whom, on the Tyrrhene seas, the tempests met,
The sailors mastered and the ships o'erset.
Amid the spirits Palinurus pressed,
Yet fresh from life, a new-admitted guest,
Who, while he steering viewed the stars, and bore
His course from Afric to the Latian shore,
Fell headlong down. The Trojan fixed his view,
And scarcely through the gloom the sullen shadow knew.

He saw also others, whom he had known on earth. Passing on, he came to the "mournful fields;" a place so called because it is the sequestered and quiet abode of those who were crossed in love, and who had pined away and died under the blight of unrequited affection.

Procris, Eriphyle here he found,
Baring her breast, yet bleeding with the wound
Made by her son.

In all his representations, he speaks of those whom he meets in the shades after their station and manner of life here upon earth. Even the kind of death they died is often alluded to. Dido is not only addressed as a queen, but is also pictured as standing before him,

"Fresh from her wounds, her bosom bathed in blood."

In like manner, Deiphobus, the son of Priam, is seen covered with his wounds, and despoiled of his limbs.

The following quotation affords a fine specimen of the ready manner in which he recognized his friends, and how similar their intercourse was to what they had been accustomed to in this world:

> He, with his guide, the farther fields attained,
> Where, severed from the rest, the warrior souls remained.
> Fidens he met, with Meleager's race,
> The pride of armies, and the soldier's grace;
> And pale Adrastus, with his ghastly face.
> Of Trojan chiefs he viewed a numerous train,
> All much lamented, all in battle slain—
> Glaucus and Medon, high above the rest,
> Antenor's sons, and Ceres' sacred priest,
> And proud Idæus, Priam's charioteer,
> Who shakes his empty reins, and aims his airy spear.
> The gladsome ghosts in circling troops attend,
> And with unwearied eyes behold their friend;
> Delight to hover near, and long to know
> What business brought him to the realms below.

Virgil also represents immediate recognition as taking place with equal ease in the highest heaven, as in the lower and more sombre Hades. Passing on through gloomy and cheerless shades, the region of those who are only partially blest, they enter at length the "verdant fields" of the higher and happier regions. Here, too, he recognizes those he knew upon the earth.

> Here found they Teucer's old heroic race,
> Born better times, and happier years of grace.
> Assaracus and Ilus here enjoy
> Perpetual fame, with him who founded Troy.

4

Still he is not satisfied. There are ties of kindred, too, and he feels himself pressed in heart to seek his relatives. He longs especially to see his father Anchises! The Sibyl makes inquiry of sacred priests and poets for the venerable hero. Kindly directed by these, they go through "blissful meadows," and find him at last in a flowery vale, viewing, with a kind of holy pride, his race of illustrious descendants, as they pass in review before him. At once old Anchises discovers his son! The scene is tender and moving! The sire sees Æneas coming, and

> Meets him with open arms and falling tears.
> "Welcome," he said, "the gods' undoubted race!
> O long-expected to my dear embrace!"

This rapture of meeting is warmly and affectionately reciprocated by the son. Is it not exactly what we feel to be natural, when, after a long separation, we meet our friends in realms of bliss? Æneas exclaims with holy joy,

> Reach forth your hand, oh parent shade! nor shun
> The dear embraces of your loving son!
> He said: and falling tears his face bedew:
> Then thrice around his neck his arms he threw!

Such were the views of this Roman poet concerning the life after death. Thus did he cheer and comfort his own heart, and the hearts of those for whom he sang, in the dark hour of bereavement and sorrow. They endured the short separation from their friends in the patience of hope. They suffered not death to break the ties which joined them to their friends. They loved the dead even as the living; yea, sometimes more — even to deification. They cherished their memories, praised their virtues, forgot their failings, and waited in the lonely longings of warm affection to meet them again in the vale of Tempe, in the Hesperian Gardens, the Elysian Fields, or in the peaceful Islands of the blest, in far-off and quiet seas.

Among modern pagans, this precious and consoling belief in the future recognition of friends is still held and cherished. The ills of life, the pangs of death, and the long, leaden hours of separation, are still softened among them by the blessed hope of reunion in a world where they die no more. The custom to which we have already alluded as existing among ancient pagans, of women, slaves, subjects and friends, killing themselves, that they might follow those to whom they were attached in life, still prevails; and it points plainly to the fact, that the belief in future recognition and eternal friendships has a deep hold upon their minds and hearts. This practice continues, according to Dr. Leland, to this day, "in Japan, Macassar, and other places. It is said to be a custom in Guinea, that when a king dies many are slain, and their bloody carcases buried with him, that they may again live with him in another world. It was formerly a well-known custom in the East Indies for women to kill themselves after the death of their husbands, that they might accompany them in the next life. And so lately as the year 1710, when the prince of Morava, on the coast of Coromandel, died, aged above eighty years, his wives, to the number of forty-seven, were burned with his corpse. We are told also that in Terra Firma, in

America, it was customary, when one of their caciques died, for his chief servants, men and women, to kill themselves, to serve him in the other world; and they buried with them maize and other provisions for their subsistence. And it is said concerning the disciples of Foe in China, that some of them, when they meet with obstacles to their passions (affections), go together to hang or drown themselves, that, when they rise together again, they may become husband and wife." True, this is ill-directed affection; and it is because it is not enlightened and sanctified by the light and spirit of a true revelation, that it leads to such sad results; but surely the strength and sincerity of it cannot be better shown than it is in this willingness to die that its possessors may follow the object they love and adore.

This precious faith in future recognition also manifests itself among modern pagans in other and lovelier forms. "Travellers tell us that the Brazilians also console themselves on the death of their friends by the hope of being united again to them, and are accustomed to express, in their lamentations, the confident expectation of seeing them in the unknown regions beyond the mountains which skirt their horizon, to renew the accustomed pleasures of the chase, the dance, and the song. So also the poor Indian of our western wilds stretches forth his hands with joy towards the world beyond his blue mountains, where he anticipates the renewal of his existence in the society of kindred and contemporary chieftains, and where he expects that even

"His faithful dog shall bear him company."

So when the wretched sons of Ham are torn, by monsters in human shape, from their home and kindred, and sold to masters in distant lands, what is their comfort, while memory, reverting to the scenes of youth, brings the tear of sorrow down their sable cheeks, but the cherished belief that after death will be formed anew those social bonds which infernal cruelty had dared to sever? This revives their spirit, and sweetens their bitter cup of life. They hope to meet their loved ones again in unmolested realms of happiness, where

> No fiends torment, nor Christians thirst for gold.

This, when far from home, is their song of rapture — this is the theme of their consolation, as they sit by the waters of captivity and weep."

> 'Tis but to die, and then to weep no more,
> Then will he wake on Congo's distant shore;
> Beneath his plantain's ancient shade renew
> The simple transports that with freedom flew;
> Catch the cool breeze that musky evening blows,
> And quaff the palm's rich nectar as it flows;
> The oral tale of elder times rehearse,
> And chant the rude traditionary verse,
> With those, the loved companions of his youth,
> When life was luxury, and friendship truth.

Such is the sighing of the pagan heart. So heave the heavy, wo-pressed bosoms of those whose infinite longings have not yet seen the star of the Christian's hopes arise in the dark firmament which overhangs the shades of moral death. Such is the "earnest expectation of the creature" stumbling in painful yet hopeful uncertainty in the way of its desires and wants. There is to us something sweetly interesting and instructive in these ideas of a future life, and the mutual recognition of friends in that life, as found among the thick gloom of paganism. It is, as already hinted, a prophecy of the truth. Just as sacrifices, which are every where resorted to in pagan religion to reconcile men with gods, proclaim the necessity of that sacrifice which Christianity reveals as an atonement for sin, so do those hopes and longings after reunion with departed friends prophetically proclaim that God will graciously provide for the full satisfaction of this want in the future inheritance of the saints.

It makes us feel happy also to think how precious must have been the drop of consolation, which this faith in future recognition afforded to those among them who sorrowed after departed friends. How merciful is God even to human infirmities; and how true is it that his tender mercies are over all his works in all places of his dominion! He pities even the poor benighted pagan, and, although he gives the children bread, he denies not to them the crumbs which fall from the table. How many tears did this faith wipe away! how many sad and forlorn spirits did it calm and cheer! and what a hopeful vista did it open to bereaved and bleeding hearts beyond the otherwise cheerless grave! Let us bless God for every drop of consolation which this doctrine has afforded to poor sorrowing heathen in the hour of fresh bereavements.

Then, too, these views are creditable to human friendship, even where it is only human. Glad are we, in this fallen world, amid the disorganizing and dividing influences of sin, to see hearts thus clinging to each other through life, and refusing even to be hopelessly sundered in death. These tendrils of living affection are like flowery vines that grow over doleful ruins to hide their hideousness, and to make the world more beautiful. Oh! why should not this be prophetic of the final and eternal renovation of our social life in heaven, where the ruins of the fall shall be restored, and where all that sin has divided shall be brought together again into the joyful embraces of holy love. We find it hard to consider a doctrine so full of consolation, and so creditable to true friendship, as only

"The herald of a lie."

We find it hard to believe that this agreeable hope, which rises like a May sun over the world of social life, cheering and warming and making it beautiful, and which often sets in richest glory, shall be finally and for ever lost in night. No—it will surely rise again in new beauty, when the eternal morning shall dawn upon the grave; holy affections, as well as glorious bodies, shall come forth from the tomb; suspended ties of affection, which, like plants whose life retired during winter into the bosom of the earth, will revive in vernal loveliness, and bloom on in an eternal spring.

In this connection, it occurs to me that there are sceptics in the world in these last days! Sceptics, who profess to regard with cold and stoic indifference all hopes and fears in reference to a future life. They boast of following the dictates of nature, reason, and the intuitive motions of an inward sense. Here, in these pagan ideas, is nature uttering its desires, its hopes, its wants, its fears — here is a voice from the deeps of burdened hearts, strong as humanity, under the pressure of infinite wants, can utter; and what does it proclaim, but the truth so plainly revealed in God's word, that the infinite longings of the human heart can find no full satisfaction on this side of an immortal life! This solemn and important truth the heart of every modern sceptic would still utter, did he not drown the voice of his own higher nature in the revilings and riotings, in the stupidity and slumbers, of earthliness and sin! Who would not be ashamed of his infidelity, when reproved by the earnest but groping heathen? Another life — and a better one — all nature proclaims. Another life — and a better one — is uttered from the constitution of our nature in the restlessness of its infinite desires. Another life — and a better one — God promises to all who will seek it by faith in Christ, who brought immortality to light. There, and there alone, are enduring treasures; there alone are joys that end not — there is life without ills, and affections that never die.

We pity the poor bewildered pagans; and it is right that we should; but let us not so misuse our superior mercies, as to give them just cause to rise up in judgment to condemn us. We enjoy superior light — let us love and use it. Let us not disgrace our faith by sorrowing for our dead even more than those who have no hope. Let our faith and hope in another life be stronger than theirs — let our affections towards our friends be holier while they are with us — let our sorrows after them be more chastened and submissive when they are taken away — let our desires after them, and the blessed inheritance upon which they have entered, be like a holy cord in our hearts to draw us away from the low delights of earth and sin — and let our gratitude to God be ardent and endless as his goodness is to us.

If we have tears to weep, let it be for the wretched on earth, and not for those who rest from their toils and woes. Weep for the dead who are dead in sin, not for the living who are alive and blest in heaven. And you, who have never been made alive in Christ Jesus, weep for yourselves. Go not to the tomb where the ashes of buried love repose — where a kindred saint sleeps in Jesus as in a downy bed—but go to the cross, and weep tears of penitence over your sins, till Jesus wipes them away.

Oh, weep not for the dead!
Rather, oh! rather give the tear
To those that darkly linger here,
When all besides are fled.
Weep for the spirit withering
In its cold, cheerless sorrowing;
Weep for the young and lovely one,
That ruin darkly revels on;
But never be a tear-drop shed
For them, the pure enfranchised dead!

CHAPTER III.

Heavenly Recognition a Universal Belief. Hope, and Desire.

I call'd on dreams and visions to disclose
That which is veiled from waking thoughts; conjured
Eternity as men constrain a ghost
T' appear and answer; to the grave I spake
Imploringly;—looked up, and asked the heavens
If angels traversed their cerulean floors,
If fixed or wandering star could tidings yield
Of the departed spirit—what abode
It occupies—what consciousness retains
Of former loves and interests.

Wordsworth, Ex. Bk. III.

THAT the saints in light shall again recognize and know each other, and renew the acquaintances and friendships formed on the earth, is a universal belief, hope and desire. Some, it is true, have affected to doubt it, and even to pretend that it is not desirable that it should be true; but not, we think, earnestly, and with a sincere and humble zeal for the truth. Any doubts which have existed in regard to this point, have, we are inclined to suppose, been the result of affectation; or, to attribute to such doubters the most charitable motives, they have been entertained under the influence of mere negative considerations. If, therefore, there are a few affected doubters, they are the exception, and not the rule; and we are not hindered in considering the desire after, and the belief in, future recognition as a universal sentiment.

A few remarks on this subject will convince any one of ordinary reflection, observation, and experience, that the hope and desire of finding again in heaven those loved and lost on earth, is strictly universal. We have seen how pagans have viewed it; we shall find it equally general in Christian lands. Not only do we find allusions to this doctrine, taking its truth for granted, among learned philosophers and theologians; but we hear of it, in like manner, among the quiet orders of common and humble life. There is not a country grave-yard, where some monumental stone does not record it, and where this hopeful thought does not prompt the rising sigh in the bosom of bereaved and sorrowing hearts, and where this sigh is not again calmed by a rising faith in this doctrine. There is scarcely a funeral discourse pronounced at the grave of the pious, in which it is not referred to in tones of sweet consolation. There is scarcely a funeral hymn in which it is not mentioned, referred to, or taken for granted. There is scarcely a death-bed around which it does not linger, like the mellow notes of a long-loved song, either on the lips of the dying, or from sympathizing friends who crowd affectionately around, to hand the departing one softly down into the Lethean stream. — Immediately after writing the last sentence, I was called, as pastor, to visit a young Sabbath-school scholar on her death-bed. She was about twelve years old, and had been much afflicted. She requested me to sing. I asked her what hymn she loved, promising to sing it. Having a few minutes before risen from my meditations on this subject, to call on her, it was a little remarkable to me that, in reply to my question, What hymn she loved? she repeated, with feeble voice and trembling lips, part of the following:

In this dark world of sin and pain,
We only meet to part again;
But when we reach the heavenly shore,
We then shall meet to part no more.
The hope that we shall see that day,
Should chase our present griefs away;
When these few years of pain are past,
We'll meet around the throne at last.

Thus, with the solemn and affectionate farewells of the pious, this faith mingles its words of hope and promise: "if we meet no more on earth, we will meet in heaven." This doctrine, also, generally closes the heart-indited letter to the absent, and is the wing of every sigh that follows them into lands distant and unknown.

The common feeling on this subject is beautifully expressed in a happy allusion to this doctrine by the late pious Dr. Nevins, in his Practical Thoughts, which will serve as a specimen of numberless others of a similar kind, abounding in biographies, obituaries, liturgies, letters, and consolatory writings. "True, death separates; but it *unites*, also. It takes us, I know, *from* many we love; but it takes us *to* as many we love." More than half of some families have gone already to heaven; why should we be so much more desirous of continuing with that part on earth, than of joining that portion which is in heaven?

So general is this belief, that it is confined to no age of the world, but is found in all ages. It is confined to no place, but is found in all places. It is peculiar to no denomination of Christians, and to no tribe, nation, or religion of pagans; but is found among all. The learned also have it even as the ignorant, and cherish it with the same implicit tenderness and affection. Like the partings and bereavements which call it forth, it is extensive as our death-doomed and dying race. "It is the voice of nature, proclaiming in loud and joyous accents the destiny of her virtuous children."

Not only is this a common and general faith, but it is associated also with a warm and animated desire. It is not a cold and dead notion by which this doctrine is held; but it is a faith that lives, and longs ardently for its realization. All most devoutly desire it to be true, and daily live on its happy and consoling promises. The bare thought that it might not be true is dreadfully distressing, and every passing doubt of its truth brings a moment's misery into the heart where it finds entrance.

The general existence, then, of this faith, and the general desire that it may be true, are undoubted. Now the question arises, How does this furnish any evidence that it is true? We will answer.

Where is there an universal idea that is not true? Where are there universal hopes or fears that are groundless? Where is there an idea that is common to heathen, Mahomedan, Jew, and Christian—common to all sects and divisions of religionists — common to high and low, learned and ignorant — common also to all lands and all ages—where is there such a universal idea of any kind, that is not founded in truth? There is none. Error alone is sectional — the catholic and universal is true. Humanity does not lie. Any want which it expresses is a true want. Any hope which it cherishes in its broad and universal bosom, is a hope that may be realized by all such as can find the path; and any fear which it feels and expresses, is no groundless fear. The heathen motto "VOX POPULI, VOX DEI," is not true, indeed, according to the sense attached to it by those who used it; but it is true in the deeper sense above explained. "The deepest lore is the most universal." The loudest and strongest testimony to truth, next to the voice from heaven, is that which heaves up mightily from the broad bosom of humanity, like the voice of one lost in a wilderness, plaintive and tremulous — the lips of the sage always tremble and utter feebly — but hopeful still. When heaven speaks, earth returns the echo; and if we hear but the echo, we know what the voice spake, though it be less distinctly. The reflected heavens in the waters of earth, preach of the heavens that are over them; and the stars that shine reflected out of their tossed and restless waves, would not be there if they were not first in the tranquil heavens above. So, what we hear sounding forth in a universal voice from the whole race of man, has been spoken to them from heaven, though in a voice so still, that only those who hold their breath in quiet hear it. There be prophets in our inner life, as well as in our outer world!

That these universal ideas are often faint, flickering, and unsteady, is not owing to the serene and unclouded firmament of truth in which they have their source and home, but to the restless medium through which they pass, and the tarnished surface in man's darkened mind from which they are reflected. Though tossed and wandering, it is still truth,

> As sunshine broken in a rill,
> Though turned astray, is sunshine still!

That all universal ideas are true, not indeed always in their form, but in their substance, may be farther established and illustrated by reference to several such. The belief in the existence of a God, for instance, is common to all men. There are no human beings to be found, however rude or polite, who do not hope or fear it. Some nations, it is true, have lost His unity, and represent Him in broken fragments; some have very wrong, and many more, very imperfect ideas of Him; but of the existence of some Sovereign Power over them, none doubt—but fools! Ps. xiv. 1. With all, the idea of God's existence is not so much a deduction of reason, as a spontaneous feeling or consciousness. It is the light and life of God's reflected image in man. He "glasses Himself" in man's spirit. He speaks forth his own existence from out the consciousness of all men whom he has made. He looks forth from his own image in man, in feeble, mellow, but yet in true manifestation. The distortions into which this truth has fallen, do not invalidate its verity—though they may obscure it—any more than fragments disprove a whole from which they are broken. The *many* gods of the heathen are fragments of the *one* true God—they prove His existence. Here, then, is an undoubted instance of the truth of an universal idea.

Alike universal, though fragmentary, is the doctrine of immortality. All men, unless they are spoiled by a vain philosophy, believe in a future state. This is generally received, and properly too, as a proof that there is another life. If the belief in an immortal state were a deduction of reason, it would never have been universal—for where is there a truth that can only be reached by reason, which is universal?—but being the result of human spontaneiety, it is broad as humanity itself. This corresponds exactly with the facts as furnished by the history of this doctrine. It was not received by those who held it through reason; but it came to them by tradition from the morning twilight of time. The fact is, reasoning on it led them away from it into doubts and fears. The more human reason was developed in the minds of pagan philosophers, and the more it sought to take this doctrine exclusively under its care, for the purpose of placing it on solid ground, the more was it lost to them in doubt and despair. The universal tradition, as it lived hopefully in the hearts and in the simple faith of the common people, was stronger and less disturbed than it was in the minds of those who sought to unfold, establish, and beautify it, in the light of reason. It is a fact which strikingly confirms what has now been said, that the doctrine of the soul's immortality was never more doubted than in the politest ages and circles of Grecian cultivation. Even Plato and Socrates, in their last hours, refreshed their fainting faith in it, not by calling to mind their own reasonings on the subject, but from the far-back fountains of sacred tradition. "They say it is true," was a stronger voice of consolation to them, than "I have reasoned that it is true."

In regard, then, to both these doctrines — viz., the existence of God, and the soul's immortality—it is the universal voice, which forms the firmest basis, out of the Bible, for the soul's repose in them. Humanity is no lie, exclaims the earnest, truth-seeking spirit; and its voice, where it gives but one sound, speaks not error, but truth.

If we need any additional proof that the deepest lore is the most universal, and that all universal ideas are true, we might refer to the universal sense of sin, the necessity of redemption, and the necessity of some atonement by sacrifice and blood! Are not these ideas everywhere found? Do they not form the very substance of all religious feelings among pagans? and are they not voices in all parts of the heathen wilderness prophetic of the coming truth? In short, there is not one vital truth in divine revelation concerning the whole race of man, that has not its likeness, though in mournful caricature and hideous burlesque, in the religious ideas of pagans. This proves beyond all doubt, that, though the reason and logic of fallen humanity are false, its sighs are true. The infinite wants which lie in their constitution reach after the truth. They seek, if haply they might feel after and find it. "For we know that the whole creation groaneth and travaileth in pain together until now."

Now, the doctrine we are discussing stands in the

same category with these universal ideas just mentioned. What has been said of them, is equally true of this. It belongs, like them, to those universal truths which spring up spontaneously from all hearts, in all ages, places, and circumstances; and, like them, it is not doubted, except where persons have overcome their spontaneous and instinctive feelings by false philosophy, by rationalistic sophisms, and by casting up difficulties and objections against it, without giving due weight to positive considerations and implicit faith. This doctrine has as deep a necessity as that of the doctrine of a future life itself; for, that man is a social being, is just as deeply grounded in his nature as that he is an immortal being, or even as deeply as the feeling that he is a being at all. Why then should not the universal belief that the doctrine of future recognition is true, be taken as a real prophecy of its truth? The universal belief in its truth, and the universal desire that it may be true, show that there is a want of it in our nature. They show that it is not a conclusion from premises that might be false, but a free instinctive testimony of nature, spontaneous and disinterested. We get it not first "by any elaborate instructions, or dint of argument, or any long train of consequences; but it strongly masters our understandings by its native evidence, and springs up in us an unpremeditated resolve."

These considerations, however, though to a reflecting mind of the deepest force, may not carry with them the convictions of most persons, as readily as some others which shall follow. If the mere fact that this faith in future recognition—like that in the existence of God, the soul's immortality, and the sense of guilt and need of redemption by sacrifice — is general, be taken as proof of its foundation in truth, the following several collateral considerations will increase our convictions of its truth.

I. We remark, first, that although the belief in this doctrine is common to all, yet it grows in the mind and heart, and becomes firm in proportion as Christianity prevails.

Where religion flourishes most, there this belief is most firmly held, and most warmly cherished. This will not be disputed. It is not so with error; though long held and ardently loved, it always grows faint and feeble in the light of Christianity, and finally vanishes entirely. If this belief were a gross pagan error, it would have shared the same fate, amid the progress of Christian light and truth. It could not have lived in the radiance of revelation. It has, however, been just the exact reverse. It has not only lived in the bright blaze of divine revelation, but it has actually grown bright and lovely in its brightness. Error may be compared to the mists of earth, which pass away before the rising sun; but truth, to plants which are warmed and cheered by its rays, which bask joyfully in its beams, and receive from its influence new beauty and perfection. So has it been with this doctrine. It has grown lovely, consistent, and more than ever desirable, as Christianity has aroused the hopes of men, enlarged their conceptions of the destiny of their own spirits, and pointed them to the joyous inheritance of an endless life.

II. Not only, generally, has this belief in future

recognition increased with the progress of religion, and been most consistent and desirable where religion was most honored; but it also grows strong in individual hearts in proportion as they grow in grace.

Those who are most deeply imbued with the spirit of Christ, hold most warmly to it. It grows with their spiritual growth, brightens with their hopes, and strengthens with their strength. Why is this so, if it be error? Is it not the Holy Spirit of truth which enlightens and sanctifies the Christian's heart? Are not the changes wrought in the soul, wrought by Him? Does not He work in them heavenly graces? Does not He guide them into all truth, and cleanse them from error? and, though He makes no new revelations to them, yet does He not show them of the things of Christ? unfold in their hearts divine truth in all its enlighteing and comforting bearings and details? If these are His workings in the heart, could this faith in future recognition grow and increase under His influence if it were an error? Would it not wax faint, and vanish away as fast as the Spirit wrought truth into the heart as a sanctifying element to free it from all error? Verily, it would. The very fact, therefore, that this doctrine gains a firmer hold in the heart while the Spirit is doing His work of grace there, proves that He cherishes it, and that it is therefore not error, but truth. If this conclusion is not admitted, we charge the Spirit of truth with begetting error, and the Spirit of comfort with encouraging dependence upon a vain consolation. We tremble at such a thought.

III. This belief is also more firmly held by saints than by sinners.

The wicked, though they perhaps all profess to believe this doctrine, nevertheless hold it, as they do all revealed truth, in a kind of practical unbelief. It never acquires the same force or preciousness in their minds and hearts, as it does in the case of Christians. How careless and thoughtless generally are unregenerate men on this subject! When one of their friends dies with the Christian's hope, it would be to them intolerable to think that this is an eternal separation, as long as they remain in their sins, if a sense of future recognition were alive in their hearts; but, though they know themselves to be sinners, and the departed one to have been pious, and hence to have gone whither they cannot come, yet how little practical effect has it upon them! It is an event that makes a transient impression, and passes in a day! They do not *feel* that this is *to them* an eternal separation; and yet such is the truth; but they *would* feel it, were this faith in future recognition deeply set in their hearts. This shows how faint, shallow, and floating, are their views and feelings in reference to it.

It is not so on the part of Christians. They feel deeply and long the absence of Christian friends who have died in the Lord. They long after them with a kind of holy impatience, till ofttimes the strength of their sorrow draws them sooner after the departed ones into the tomb—and into Heaven! We can only account for the fact that this belief is stronger in saints than in sinners, on the ground that the same grace and the same Spirit's influences, which sanctify the heart, also encourage it in this precious faith. This could, however, not be the case, were it not founded in truth.

IV. Not only is this faith more operative in Christians than in sinners, but it is most active in the hearts of Christians themselves in the time of their deepest sorrows.

When the darkness of their souls is greatest, on account of the loss of those whom religion itself taught them to love more than they could have loved them without it—when they sit dumb and silent in grief, this thought comes and looks forth smilingly upon them, like the cheering light of hope from behind the clouds of despair. The consolation of this doctrine comes, with a strength and sweetness which it has not at any other time, in the night-time of loneliness and bereavement—just when it is most needed. When evening comes—and to whom does it not come?—then do dark clouds gather around the gloomy portals of closing day; yet the sun behind them, out of sight, it is true, but still shining, opens up golden vistas between them, like gates of light, into a brighter heaven beyond; so, when the friendly orbs around which our affections circled, and which were the light and joy of our souls, sink beneath the horizon of earth, the belief in a heavenly recognition forms inlets, through which the love-light of the departed still streams back into our sad hearts, and gives us promise of a brighter morrow. A soothing voice, deep in the forlorn spirit, seems to say,

> Be still, sad heart, and cease repining;
> Behind the cloud is the sun still shining.

Thus, while sitting, bereaved and mournful, under the willows, where the stream of mortal life flows sighing, we are comforted. Why is this source of consolation so peculiarly refreshing just at this time? Is the Holy Spirit "the Comforter," who abides with us always? and has He nothing to do with the light of comfort which thus arises in our hearts from this doctrine in our darkest hours? Yea more, does He at this time allow our hearts to be deceived into quietude by the sweetness of a lie? Or does He mock our sorrows by a consolation which will only end in dreary disappointment? God forbid! The thought of it, if seriously entertained, is not far short of blasphemy.

These considerations, it seems to me, must have great force to a reflecting mind. We see that effects are produced by this doctrine, that can only be produced by the Holy Spirit's co-operation; we must, therefore, conclude that it has His sanction, and must be true.

Not only do we derive a proof in favor of this doctrine from the universal belief that it is true, but also from the universal *desire* that it may be true.

We do not suppose, let it be remembered, that the mere fact that this desire exists in the minds of *some* men is of itself a satisfactory proof that it is true. This desire might be awakened in some by earnest speculation on the subject—it might spring out of the imperfection of human knowledge, or out of wrong ideas of heavenly felicity: yea, even out of the natural heart entirely; for low sensualists, and even refined ones, may look for sensual delights in heaven, and may even ardently desire them; but this is no proof that they will be found there. We say, therefore, that the mere fact that this desire exists in the hearts of some, is of itself no satisfactory evidence that it will ever be realized. It is quite different, however, when this desire is universal, as it is in this case. Then it is the voice of nature, of which God himself is the author, under the pressure and sense of its own wants, proclaiming with undivided testimony what those wants are, and what will satisfy them. Men, for some self-interest, may delude themselves, may create wants, and then seek to have them satisfied; but these will always be sectional and limited: a want like this, which is universal, is different. It is the simple, spontaneous utterance of nature, unsophisticated and free — nature instinctively groaning, painfully but hopefully, in the direction of its destiny, and reaching earnestly forward to feel its way into rest and peace.

As in the case of an universal belief, so also in the case of an universal *desire*, this fact, in connection with other facts, which naturally grow out of this and are associated with it, afford a strong proof of the truth of the doctrine of future recognition.

Thus, the fact that this desire, though universal, is strongest where Christianity prevails most, and increases as our spirits grow in the Christian life — just as the belief in it grows with growth in grace — is evidence beyond doubt that this desire is founded in Christian truth. If the Holy Spirit sanctifies and increases these desires while He is performing his gracious work in the heart — which he does, as is shown by the fact that they do increase in proportion as the work of sanctification goes on—then they are surely founded in real want, and will certainly be satisfied in a complete realization. The Spirit does not induce us to cherish desires, and Himself strengthen them, for the full satisfaction of which there is not complete provision made in those rich consolations which He has in store for all God's dear children. If He did this, he would work on the soul for a false issue. He would be triflng with our spirits; yea, even with our sorrows! He would be only mocking us, while leading us forth with comforting words to fearful and bitter disappointment! This, the Comforter, the Spirit of all truth, will not do. No. When we have been long absent from our homes and friends, the desire to see them grows stronger, the nearer we draw towards them; so, the farther we proceed on the heavenly way, under the guidance of the Comforter, towards those who are now "saints in light," the more does our desire to join them increase. Which now is most reasonable to believe, that the Holy Spirit increases this pious desire to make the disappointment more bitter, or to make the joyful meeting more ecstatic? I have asked, and thou shalt answer me.

We have now seen that the hope, belief, and desire of future heavenly recognition, are universal; we have also seen in what way this fact furnishes a strong ground in which to rest the belief that it is a true doctrine. We cannot help observing in what an interesting light this fact places the whole human family before our view. Various as men are in their religious, civil and social characters, and in their positions and circumstances in life, all fondly cling to this hope. In this, high and low, rich and poor, bond and free, Christians and pagans, all agree. The king upon his throne, and the beggar weary beside the highway, equally desire this boon. In this the most learned theologian, and the most ignorant pagan, are of one mind. It is strange, if this be error, that amid such a variety there should not be some whose hearts and minds could surmount it, and cast the delusion in hatred away.—What is most interesting in this view, is the reflection: What a leveller is truth, especially the truths of the other world! All who embrace them must step down upon the same humble level. Where are earth's aristocratic distinctions in the light of eternity? At the well of Jacob, Christ the Great, and the Samaritan woman alike quench their thirst—like that well are the fountains of consolation which God opens up from the future life; here all who will drink must meet. The king may dip with a golden goblet, and the beggar with a gourd; but the water is the same to both. Where is your greatness, ye proud ones? Where is your royalty, ye of the princely line? Where are your titles, ye élite of the earth? Your hope of eternal blessedness is a hope to sit with a "beggar in Abraham's bosom." Bring your crowns, your sceptres, your diadems, and all your royal toys, ye great ones—lay them down at the feet of our common Saviour,

"And crown Him Lord of all."

The fact of the universality of this doctrine, as just discussed, is interesting, also, in teaching us that there are yet universal ideas in this world of fragments. Humanity, and human hopes and fears, are still one. In all its variety and diversity, there remains, nevertheless, a blessed unity. It proclaims itself as one, if not in its conflicting interests, still in its wants and wishes. Its misery is one; its bereavements are alike, and it partakes of one sorrow. The world, then, can still sit together, if at no other time, when it weeps! If we come not together in our faith, we do in our hopes. If we cannot meet in the house of praise, prayer and worship, we do meet in the house of mourning. This should teach us to cultivate the sweet and tender sympathies of an universal charity.

It is a refreshing thought to us, that, in the midst of the almost endless perplexities of fragmentary ideas and cold negatives, there are still some positive bonds of universal and eternal fellowship. We testify to this by the tears of our common grief. In this sphere our sympathies are truly catholic. All weep over broken ties; these ties, therefore, concern all. He that mourns —and who mourns not—is our brother! Let us seek to draw more closely to each other in all respects. Let our common woes, our common love, and our common sorrow for the dead, teach us to lay aside all selfishness—to cultivate common interests, and common sympathies. In our graves we shall be one, and alike! The kingdom of the dead is a catholic kingdom—all lie low in the dust.

"Their hatred and their envy is now perished."

Here we meet, both in our affections and in our final condition. Let us learn, therefore, to love the living as we love the dead. Why should we cherish so fondly our love for the departed, and desire that our relations to them may not be broken for ever, and not learn to draw closer those ties which lie so near to us among all the living? For this purpose, God breaks our hearts into tenderness and tears, by a common sorrow, that our affections may

> Like kindred drops be mingled into one.

Shame on our religion, that we meet not, unless we flow together on the stream of our mutual tears!—but better thus than not at all.

This universal desire after a heavenly recognition, then, besides affording us a precious argument in favor of its truth, teaches us, also, that all the hatred, divisions, and conflicts in our race, are against nature, as well as against God's will, and the spirit of our holy religion. Nature, from its broad bosom, in its common hopes and fears, proclaims the human race a brotherhood. The cord of love, however, that should run through humanity, alas! is broken. Let us seek to restore it. This we can only do by imbibing the life and love of that revelation in which both the true relations of life in this world, and the blessedness of love's immortality, are brought to light. As we expect to be eternally near each other in the upper kingdom of love, let us begin to draw the cords closer on earth. Let us long to have broken ties mended, even as we long to have existing ones to last for ever. In Christ, and in him alone, can our race, long divided and estranged by sin, be brought together. He is lifted up that he may draw all men unto Him. To Him shall the gathering together of the people be. Those who are united to him in life and love, will be united also to each other here in this world through life, and in heaven eternally. In Him,

The saints on earth, and all the dead,
  But one communion make;
All join in Christ, their living Head,
  And of his life partake.

In such society as this,
  My weary soul would rest;
The man that dwells where Jesus is,
  Must be for ever blest.

CHAPTER IV.

Heavenly Recognition in the light of Reason.

All love believes in a double immortality—in its own, and in that of the object it loves. When love once fears that it may cease, it has already ceased. It is all the same to our hearts whether the beloved one fades away, or only his love.

JEAN PAUL.

IT has by some been thought necessary to raise several distinct questions in regard to future recognition, so as to place it in a reasonable light. By some there has been "a great gulf fixed"—not between the saved in heaven and the lost in hell, where God has fixed it, but between the abode of the saints before the resurrection and after it. Some deny that, as taught in the Heidelberg Catechism, "the soul after this life shall be *immediately* taken up to Christ its head"—some deny that, as taught in the Shorter Catechism, "the souls of believers are at their death made perfect in holiness, and do *immediately* pass into glory"—some deny that, as taught in the Westminster Confession, the souls of believers are at death immediately "received into the highest heavens." Instead of this consoling doctrine, the existence of a "*middle place*" is imagined, where the spirits of the saints are detained until they receive their bodies. Hence it has been thought necessary, in proper respect to this imagination, to inquire whether recognition will take place among disembodied spirits in this "middle place" before the resurrection. As to the intermediate or disembodied condition of the saints, we will presently give answer. The existence, however, of any such middle place, we deny. It has no foundation either in reason, scripture, or the teachings of the Church, except where these have been made to speak under the influence of pagan philosophy. This, however, is not the place to discuss this question.*

If there is no intermediate place, there is, nevertheless, an intermediate condition. This may still seem to leave behind it a difficulty. Even if the spirits of the saints at death, "being then made perfect in holiness, are received into the highest heavens," still, being disembodied, there may seem to be difficulties in the way of recognition which will not exist after the resurrection. Still, I see no reason why this should be a separate question; for, so far as the scripture evidence which is brought forth on this subject bears upon future recognition *in general*, we have just the same reason to believe that it will take place before the resurrection as after it. The Scriptures plainly make no distinction of this kind. The only thing, then, necessary to be determined, is, whether there are any insurmountable difficulties from the side of reason lying against it, which would demand a separate discussion of these

---

* The grounds on which the existence of a middle place is denied are given in the author's work entitled, "Heaven, or an Earnest and Scriptural Inquiry into the Abode of the Sainted Dead;" where this subject is discussed at length. To it the reader is referred.

questions If no such difficulties exist, it may remain to us *one* question, as the Scriptures have made it.

Do any such difficulties exist? To this we answer, that the idea of future recognition, even among disembodied spirits, is not unreasonable. Even if it were above reason, it might not be against it; but it is not even above reason: for we know that there are peculiarities of spirit, peculiarities of intellectual faculties and of moral dispositions, which mark the identity and difference of beings, and which distinguish them from each other, just as clearly and tangibly as they are distinguished by any peculiarities of body. By these, recognition is possible. In the future world, before the resurrection, where spirits meet spirits without the intervention of the body, these peculiarities of spirit may be even more prominent and striking than any peculiarities of the body can possibly be; and thus, instead of hindering, may greatly facilitate mutual recognition.

There is, moreover, reason to believe that, among the bright and sinless hosts of heaven, there are spirits who know and recognize each other, without any of those coarse and sensible marks of identity which are here in this life furnished by our intervening bodies. There is therefore nothing unreasonable in the idea of mutual recognition among the saints in their disembodied state before the resurrection of the body. Hence we must give the Scriptures, which, so far as they throw light upon this subject, make no distinction of the kind and no division of the subject, their full weight and their greatest latitude.

It has also by some been thought necessary to determine or inquire whether future recognition will take place at once, and *on sight*, as we now recognize an old acquaintance whom we unexpectedly meet in a strange city or country; or whether it will take place gradually, by converse and intercourse, which will at length lead to the mutual discovery that there was a previous acquaintance, just as we sometimes, in old age, meet a friend that we had not seen since youth, and with whom we gradually revive old associations. Here, again, we see not the necessity of looking at these two ideas as two questions which need separate discussion and inquiry. Recognition will no doubt take place in both these ways, just as it does in this world. We love to look at the other world as having the same social features as this; and there is no Scripture and no reason that forbids it. We shall doubtless be more surprised to find the social aspects of the other life so much like this, than we shall be to find it so different.

In those "heavenly pastimes," we may suppose some sudden and joyful surprises, in cases where one shall at once recognize his friends, and he not be at once recognized by them. Kindred may meet, as the sons of Jacob met Joseph in Egypt, and, while regarding each other as strangers, a sudden joyful melting of hearts may be produced by some such expression as—"I am Joseph your brother!" Again, there may be meetings in which a gradual recognition will take place, like that of the two disciples who fell in with Christ, after his resurrection, on their way to Emmaus. At first when he joined himself to their company, their "eyes were holden" that they did not know Him; but after some conversation with them by the way, in which he entered into the subject of their thoughts in regard to "the things which had happened at Jerusalem," and especially after they came to Emmaus, while he sat at meat with them, and "took bread, and blessed it, and brake, and gave to them," which brought to their minds the scene of the last supper, behold! "their eyes were opened, and they knew Him!' Here, associations gradually waked up in their minds and hearts the remembrance of their Lord, and with these returned to their recollection his familiar features. So in the heavenly world, beyond doubt, there will be a great variety of ways in which old associations and acquaintanceships will be revived; some sudden and joyful to ecstacy — others gradual, but none the less pleasant on that account. Some may take place through the kind ministry of friendly angels, and others through the affectionate agency of saintly spirits. In whatever way, and by whatever means it may take place, it is in entire accordance with reason, and just what we might suppose to be natural and proper to that social kingdom in our Father's house, in the everlasting home of the Sainted Dead.

In considering farther, and more particularly, the reasonableness of this doctrine, we do not intend to confine ourselves to deduction of pure reason, but shall present such inferences and conclusions as may be legitimately drawn from known facts, whether in Scripture or experience. It must be remembered that reason at present lives in the light of revelation, and must be so viewed. From some truths revealed in the Scriptures, though not directly on this subject, we may nevertheless deduce arguments in favor of this doctrine, which show it to be so reasonable as strongly to prepossess our minds towards it. This will be of vast account in the way of preparing our minds to consider it in its scriptural light.

I. This doctrine of future recognition is reasonable, because many of the same means which will enable us to identify ourselves in another life, will also enable us to identify our friends and former acquaintances.

When we awake from the swoon or sleep of death, or emerge through the change of death into the realities, circumstances, and affinities of another life, we suppose our first feeling will be that of consciousness of our own identity. We will feel and be conscious that we are ourselves, and not another. This we can only do in connection with our past history. It may be the work of an instant; but still it involves a process by which the mind connects itself with what is past, and recollects its previous existence. Thus, for instance, we spend a night in the house of a friend; we wake in the morning suddenly, and scarcely know where we are, or who we are. The mind at once enters upon a process of discovery by self-recollection: to do this, it goes back and calls up its past history, remembers the way in which it has come, and, soon, full consciousness of itself and its relations is restored. So, in the other world, after the change of death, a consciousness of identity must in some such way be continued. Suppose, however, that in the case of the person just instanced, sleeping in the house of his friend, the room should be furnished in a certain way when he lay down to sleep, and the furniture should be entirely removed and changed while he slept; the difficulty in coming to a consciousness of his identity would be greatly increased. In that case it would be necessary for him to depend upon pure recollection of the past in the way of thought and memory. This must be the case with our souls passing the change of death; we will find ourselves in new relations, circumstances, and affinities; and our consciousness of personal identity can continue only as it feels itself the living continuation of the past. This life, with its associations, must come up before the mind and awake in the heart; and with this must appear our friends with whom we were bound up on earth by social ties and relations. Undoubtedly our social relations and dependences—for it was these that, more than anything else, moulded our life—must stand out in prominence among our first recollections, after we have passed the physical transformation which awaits us in death. This forms at least a reasonable basis for the doctrine under contemplation; nothing can well be more reasonable. Its denial, under this view, involves a violence so unheard-of and unnatural, that our reason is startled and distressed at the thought of it.

II. Closely allied to the above observations, is the fact that memory will continue in another life.

That this world is remembered in the world to come, is evident from the example of the rich man to whom father Abraham said those piercing words, "Son, remember that thou in thy *life-time!*" We are told that he did remember his "father's house," and his "five brethren!" This, it is true, was in the place of the lost; but memory being a noble faculty when rightly used, we may safely believe, with additional reasons, that it will continue among those who "shall know as they are known."* "However, I may affirm for an infallible truth," says the pious and learned Rev. Charles Drelincourt, of Paris, "that the glory of heaven, as well as grace, shall bring nature to perfection, but shall not destroy it. It shall add to it other excellences, but it shall not take away those that it hath already. It shall not abolish any of the faculties; but it shall beautify and enrich them with new ornaments. Therefore, consequently, it shall not take away our memory, which is one of the rarest gifts and abilities of the reasonable soul."

It is hard to see how memory can exist in the better world without leading to recognition. How deep-seated and precious are old associations! and how strong is our desire that they may be revived! Our friends, from a previous knowledge of their piety, and impelled by our affection for them, will be sought after; which, we may reasonably conclude, will lead to the restoration of them to us, and us to them. Desire after our friends is among the first emotions of our souls when away from them in a new country. Especially, when we are happy and they are in circumstances less blest, do we think of them. Our love to them naturally begets this feeling. We think of them, inquire after them, and long for their presence with us, that they may share our blessedness. We cannot conceive how memory can continue in heaven without leading to such results. Thus, we will not only remember this world as a means by which our identity is preserved; but we see also that there is a principle in our nature which strongly urges our thoughts backward, and sets them

* See "Heaven, or the Sainted Dead," pp. 276–282.

to seeking for those loved and left behind. All this is favorable to future recognition; and, that it is true, is the most reasonable conclusion we can arrive at. The opposite is certainly against reason and all experience.

III. This doctrine will appear reasonable when we consider how deeply and radically the social law lies imbedded in our nature.

We are created social beings, and it is in no sense good for man to be alone. We are all by nature, and in our constitution, physical, intellectual, and moral, united, related, and dependent. All disorganization and alienation is the result of sin, and in the highest degree violent and unnatural. This piety seeks to restore, whose nature and object is, to unite and bind. Christianity, coming from above into a world spoiled by the divisions which sin has caused, establishes a fellowship which is to unite us on earth, and then to raise us, thus united, into the upper kingdom of holy and eternal love. It is not reasonable that religion should form ties to be broken at death, when it comes from heaven and designs to raise us to heaven. What grace makes, is to last for ever—what grace binds, is never to be severed.

We know, moreover, that religion elevates, improves, sanctifies, and perfects true friendship. Does it do this only that death may destroy it? Ah! who can believe it? On the contrary, time only increases true attachments. In connection with the past, true friendship lives. The hallowed associations which connect it with the past are its life and its joy. Memory is the fuel of love. Old and long-remembered associations give to it its mystic sacredness. As the recollections of childhood always awaken youthful feelings in our hearts, so the remembrance of the past gives a fresh glow and a lovely tenderness to social ties. How then can true love die? Our nature must be entirely changed before its affections can cease.

If such be our social nature, it is certainly not reasonable that it, unfolded through life under these sweet relations and dependencies of earthly friendship and love, should be suddenly robbed of them in the transition of death. This would be a violence which is nowhere tolerated in the laws of life and love. We will venture the assertion that there is no law more essential to our existence, and which may not with less danger be laid aside, than this social law of love. A being that can break loose from all former ties and affectionate affinities, is that moment changed into a devil! As "God is love," and as all his attributes are connected and controlled by this — the very essence of his nature —so we, who are made in his image, are social beings necessarily. The kingdom of Christ exists on earth to redeem, preserve, and perfect our social nature, and reveal the nature of God in us; all the beginnings of it on earth are, therefore, beginnings of its heavenly perfection. The very establishment and perpetuation of Christianity on earth has been, from the first, by families, tribes, and generations; thus it laid hold of, and took up into itself at once, the elements of the world's social life, and used them in its own advancement; and it will not, it cannot, we think, cast them off in its heavenly glorification. Hence we see that Christianity, in its very essence, identifies itself with the social law and life of our nature, and makes them eternal, by making itself eternal in them. If this be so, then the ties here formed, so far as they are sanctified by Christianity, will continue uninterrupted through death, and be eternally perfecting in heaven.

Moreover, we know that *some* of the prominent ties and relations formed in the kingdom of Christ on the earth will be perpetuated. For this we have scripture proof. Christ's apostles shall sit together as judges of the twelve tribes of Israel. As to himself, his people shall see him as he is, face to face. Is it unreasonable, nay, is it not in the highest degree reasonable, that this recognition shall descend from these prominent points down into the minuter avenues and lanes of the social life of heaven? "Will not He who '*loved* Lazarus,' and who said, 'Our *friend* Lazarus sleepeth,' be recognised by Lazarus in the better world? and if he recognise his Saviour, why not also his sisters, Martha and Mary? And will not 'the disciple whom Jesus loved,' that bosom friend, recognise his Lord and Master? and if so, why not all those who sat at meat with him, when he affectionately reclined on his Redeemer?" Certainly all this is reasonable. It is difficult to see how it can be otherwise. It is much easier to believe it true than false.

IV. Death sometimes makes interruptions in the process of things which seem, in the nature of things, to require completion in a future life; which, however, can only be done by recognition.

We are, for instance, often blest in this world by a person who may never know that he has blessed us; we may be prevented, by circumstances of some kind or other, from making known to him our gratitude. Is it not, then, exceedingly probable that, in a future life, opportunity will be afforded us to acknowledge the favor with gratitude, by which both his and our own happiness would be greatly augmented? In the case of the philanthropist, it seems necessary, in order to his being rewarded according to his works, that the fruits of his labors, as they exhibited themselves unknown to him, in the happiness and salvation of others should be brought to his view, either by God or by the persons blessed; that, as part of his reward, he may review with holy satisfaction the good he has been enabled by grace to perform while on earth. This, it seems reasonable to believe, would lead to the reviving of earthly relations and associations, and thus gradually to recognition, and a renewal of former earthly acquaintance.

This is the more probable, as gratitude, in the heart of the one who receives favors, naturally produces in him a desire to express his feelings to the one who has blessed him. In the case where an individual is indebted for even the salvation of his soul to the instrumentality of one whom he is never afterwards privileged to see, will he not desire to meet him in heaven? This desire will naturally lead to a search after him, and, we may well suppose, to a meeting, and to mutual joy. What joyful meetings of this kind may take place in the heavenly world! With raptures inexpressible will those who have turned others to righteousness, find them again in the heavenly places, as their hope, their joy, and crown of rejoicing.

V The final judgment necessarily involves details

of acts of persons inseparably associated with each other, so as to lead naturally to recognition.

All our good deeds are of a social kind — a great many of our good acts are so connected with the acts of others, and their influences are so merged into each other, that even we ourselves cannot trace our own acts in all their consequences. We influence others, and they us. All the sins against the second table of the law are social sins, and cannot be referred to, in the judgment, without reference to all parties involved and implicated. So also the virtues of the second table are social virtues, and must be so disposed of, in the rewards of the judgment. Thus, in their reward, they must be associated with the persons judged, as they were associated on the earth. The judgment by which these acts are rewarded must have reference to these acts in their social character and connections. Thus, faithfulness of parents in their family duties — faithfulness on the part of the members of a congregation towards each other, and in the community generally — makes the recollection and recognition of those thus associated absolutely necessary, in the proceedings of that great day. Though the influences of social acts may be lost to us in the details of their silent, and oft-times secret consequences, yet "every man's work shall be made manifest: for the day shall declare it." We know that if the giving of a cup of cold water in the name of a disciple is rewarded in heaven, it will be done with such a reference to the saint who received the draught as will enable the one who is rewarded to recognise him. How this fact will swell the little kindnesses of earth to an exceeding weight of glory in heaven! The sensations of joy which the remembrance of such acts will produce, are not too mean to excite into higher raptures of bliss even the holy bosoms of the saints in light.

VI. The doctrine of heavenly recognition is highly reasonable to us, when we consider the ground we have for believing that our knowledge in the future world will be vastly enlarged in a general way, and of course in this respect in particular.

That our minds will be greatly enlarged in the future life, none can reasonably doubt. It is a matter of express revelation. "For we know in part, and we prophesy in part. But when that which is perfect is come, then that which is in part shall be done away. When I was a child, I spake as a child, I understood as a child, I thought as a child: but when I became a man, I put away childish things. For now we see through a glass, darkly; but then face to face: now I know in part; but then shall I know even as also I am known." 1 Cor. xiii. 9–13. The apostle's declaration, "It is sown in weakness, it is raised in power," is as much applicable to the soul as to the body. Sin has greatly obscured the mind, and partially deadened its faculties. As the Israelites could not sing in a strange land, so the human faculties cannot act with freedom and energy in the captivity of sin, and in their alienation from God; but when brought home into their proper relation to Him, they will expand into new bloom of beauty and life. In those genial climes of cloudless day, they will unfold themselves without obstruction, and without end. There, where the heart shall be pure, the mind will become clear. In the society of angels and pure spirits, and near the radiant source of all wisdom and knowledge, the human mind will, like God himself, clothe itself with light as with a garment.

It is certainly unreasonable to imagine, that while the soul makes new attainments in knowledge, it will lose and leave behind what it has already attained. Our present knowledge, so far as consistent with the divine will and wisdom, will not be destroyed, but taken up and included in our future knowledge. It is not reasonable to believe, that the attainments we have made in this life, should give us no advantage in the beginning of the life to come. This would make all our earthly tuition of no avail, and needless. If, then, our knowledge will increase in general, it must also increase in particular; and if our present knowledge will not be destroyed, but merged and included in the higher wisdom of our eternal state, it will most assuredly bear along with it that particular knowledge which is associated with the heavenly recognition of our sainted friends.

In this view, there is a good deal of sense and sound reason in the quaint and pleasant anecdote which has often been related of an old Welsh divine. One day, while pursuing his studies, his wife being in the room, she suddenly interrupted him, "John Evans, do you think we shall be known to each other in heaven?" Without hesitation, he replied, "To be sure we shall; do you think we shall be greater fools there, than we are here?" It is certainly far from wise to suppose, that it will be part of the perfection of our future state to lose that knowledge which we now have, so far as it involves no immorality.

VII. The interest which heavenly beings feel in the affairs of saints on earth, furnishes us reasonable ground for the belief in heavenly recognition.

There is no difficulty in believing that, on the part of saints in heaven, an acquaintance with us is kept up. We have lost them for a time, but they have not lost us. As they have gone higher, they have capacities and privileges which we, who are still beneath them, have not; and this may extend to a constant oversight and interest in us.* This sense is as natural as any other to the passage, "Then shall I know even as also I am known." We are now known to them; but when we enter the state in which they now are, then shall we know them as they now know us. The Old Testament saints are represented as a cloud of witnesses around us, like the crowd which bent down from all sides upon the race-ground in the Olympic games. According to this allusion of the Apostle, they are around us, not merely as examples, but as interested spectators. That we are not conscious of this, does not prove its improbability; for the lower orders of nature that are beneath us are not aware of our perfect knowledge of them, neither do they know us, and yet we know them — their nature, habits, prospects, and destiny. In like manner, we have reason, and also intimations of Scripture, to confirm in us the belief that our sainted friends are bending an interested eye of love over us in all our earthly pilgrimage — that they keep up a tender and affectionate acquaintance

* See "Heaven, or the Sainted Dead," third edition, p. 282, et seq

with us, and stand ready, when we fail on earth, to receive us into the arms of holy and eternal love, at the very gates of the heavenly paradise. Or must we believe that they are less interested in us than the rich man in hell was for his five brethren!

Even if the saints do not, and cannot behold and follow us with personal attention, they can still keep up an acquaintance with us, in our earthly history, through the angels. Angels are the constant companions of the blest in heaven; and they are also upon the earth, "ministering spirits, sent forth to minister for them who shall be heirs of salvation." In heaven they "do always behold the face" of our Father; and on earth they "encamp around our dwellings," and attend us, to "keep us in all our ways." As on Jacob's mystic ladder, they are constantly descending from heaven to earth, and ascending from earth to heaven; thus keeping alive the fellowship of love on both sides of the mysterious veil!

Can we for a moment believe that, if the saints above are still interested in us, there are no inquiries of returning angels in regard to us, and that our sainted friends do not thus keep themselves informed as to our state and life? It is not only said that angels themselves are interested in saints on earth, but that "there is joy *in the presence of* the angels of God over one sinner that repenteth." Who are these that rejoice in the presence of the angels over a converted sinner? Are they not the sainted friends of the sinner? they who, while on earth, often prayed for his conversion, and in remembrance of whose faith, and in answer to whose prayers, God has now sent forth to him His converting grace? Our relation with the spirit-world, and our participation in its sympathies, is most intimate and endearing; it is only the benumbing influence of dull sense that keeps us from feeling it. The very reverence which we feel towards the unseen spirits of the dead, proclaims the power of their influence over us. Though this feeling is dark and unintelligible to us, it is not so to them. We live in the midst, and under the constant power, of mysterious unseen influences, which strongly declare the fact, that we are in a sphere of existence influenced by a higher world, and under the attention of higher intelligences, who are ever drawing us to themselves; and, soon as the separation of soul and body — the natural and finite from the spiritual and infinite — shall take place in death, we shall discover at once how awfully and sweetly near we have always been to the dead, and how much we shared in their affectionate sympathies. It is only when the infant becomes a man, that it fully sees and knows what the mother's eyes, arms, and bosom, were to it, during its years of infantile helplessness. So, when our spirits once break through the thin veil of this imperfect earthly life, which hides the world of spirits, into the full stature of celestial manhood, they will only fully understand those influences, the good of which they have always felt. If such is the relation, and such the mutual sympathies between heaven and earth, it is in the highest degree reasonable, that the holy ties of earthly affections pass unbroken through the change of death, and revive with new strength and beauty in the upper kingdom of love.

We take great pleasure in the conclusions to which these reflections bring us. We delight greatly in the hope that the ties which bind us to our sainted friends are not broken in death — that while we are loving them still, they love us too; and while we long to find them again, they are watching with holy interest over us, and are alluring us, by sweet mysterious influences, into their holy society, and into a participation, with them, of celestial joys. Seeing we are compassed about with so great a cloud of witnesses, we are animated to lay aside every weight—even that of the body itself in death—that we may fly to their embraces, and be near them, as they are near the Lord.

CHAPTER V.

Heavenly Recognition among the Jews.

Oh, wondrous times! — those palmy days of old; —
When God with prophets spake, and angels walk'd
With men — when heaven, with mild and radiant eye,
Through dreams, and types, and shadowy visions look'd,
And smiled on all who sought a better life.
Though darkly hung the mystic veil that hid
The better world; yet, through it, faith beheld,
On the celestial side, the lovely forms
Of sainted friends in blessed pastimes move.
They mourn'd, but still in hope, for those beyond;
And, smiling through their tears, in meekness said,
They cannot come to us, but we shall go
To them.

We have discovered some beautiful glimmerings of this interesting doctrine of future recognition in the midst of pagan gloom. We have seen that it is a universal belief, hope and desire. We have also seen that it is in accordance with the dictates of enlightened reason. We come now to view it in the lovely religious twilight of Jewish hope.

It is agreed upon, by all who have earnestly reflected upon the subject, that all religious ideas among pagans may be traced back, through dim and misty tradition, to the Jews, to whom alone spiritual revelations were anciently made. The report of these revelations, though only in faint and feeble echo, reached the surrounding pagans, and waked up their hearts and minds to a sense of their wants. Around the abodes of the Patriarchs, Prophets, and Jewish people generally, the holy light of heaven shone; and though there appears also at times to be light out in the deep gloom, it is but a reflection: just as there are bright objects on the earth, though the sun is the source of their light. If, then, we are to trace the rays of light, which dart broken through the gloom of pagan night, to the sun of revelation, as it arose over the Jewish people, we may expect to find an increase of light upon this subject in Jewish ideas and theology. True, even here we expect to find this doctrine only *obscurely*, as the Jewish dispensation was one of hope—the dawn of the eternal morning. Yet we do well to look to this, as "a light that shineth into a dark place, until the day-dawn and the day-star ariseth in our hearts." Although it is shadow, and not substance, yet the shadow always gives us a correct idea of the substance, even if it be only a partial one; though it be only prophecy of what shall be, it is sure prophecy, and will lead us to a complete fulfilment. If we follow the smallest, feeblest rill, that rises in the remotest and most obscure vale of earth, it will lead us finally to the great and wide sea—it is water, small as it is; so, if we seize upon the feeblest ray of light that catches our eye in the surrounding gloom, and follow it, we come at length to the full, clear, and unclouded truth.

We shall see, I trust, in this inquiry into the Jewish ideas of recognition in another life, that the doctrine will present itself with additional clearness, preciousness and beauty, as we proceed. By tracing the doctrine in this historical way, it will not only seem more living, but also more convincing; we will be carried along by gradual degrees of evidence, and our path, like that of the just man, will shine more and more unto the perfect day.

Before we proceed to offer the proof, that the Jews believed in the doctrine of heavenly recognition, a few preparatory remarks are necessary, to open the subject properly before us. Some have strangely pretended to doubt, whether the Jews knew anything at all of another life. That their ideas on this subject were as clear and full as ours, no one will pretend; but that they had many consoling views of an immortal life, none can deny. The doctrine of immortality, like that of the existence of God, is taken for granted in the Old Testament. Rewards and punishments, the hopes and fears of the future, the eternal favour or displeasure of God, were evidently as familiar ideas among the Jews as every-day matters. As the doctrine of another life was thus taken for granted, it is rather indirectly alluded to, than directly stated. The Patriarchs and Prophets no doubt knew much more of this doctrine than is mentioned in the sacred record. God, for instance, told our first parents that if they ate of the forbidden tree, they should surely die, in *that day*. As they did not die a natural or temporal death immediately, it seems necessary, in order that they might know at all that the penalty had actually fallen upon them, that they should know something of a spiritual and eternal death. This they could not know without the doctrine of immortality. The translation of Enoch and Elijah could mean nothing to them without the knowledge of another life. Noah could not have acted the part recorded of him without reference to a recompense of reward; for, how could he be a "preacher of righteousness," without having some motive to present from another world, or without exhibiting the "end of righteousness, which is quietness and assurance for ever?" The whole, moreover, is decided by Paul, who tells us that what Noah and the Patriarchs did, they did "by faith." Faith itself implies the knowledge of a future life, for it is "the substance of things hoped for, the evidence of things not seen." To say, then, that any of the Old Testament saints had faith, is to say that they believed in the unseen realities of another life.

Our present design does not require us to pursue this part of the subject any farther. We may add, that if what has been said does not satisfy the reader on this point, he may consult the following passages of Scripture, and see whether he can afterwards doubt that the Jews knew of, and believed in, a future life. 2 Kings ii. 1—8. Job xix. 25—28. Psalms xvi. 10; xvii. 15; xlix. 15; lxxiii. 24—26. Eccl. xii. 7, 14. Isaiah xxvi. 19. Ezek. xxxvii. 1—10. Dan. xii. 1—3. Christ himself declares that Moses knew that the dead are raised. Luke xx. 38. Paul says that Abraham, and a host of others, looked for an heavenly country. Heb. xi.

This much it was necessary to say, that all doubt on this point may be removed, and that we may be convinced that the Old Testament saints felt themselves in close, warm, and living sympathy with the unseen and eternal world. Under the power and influence of this impression we will be able to see more force than we could otherwise do, in the proofs which we intend to present in favour of their belief in future heavenly recognition. It is plain, that the doctrine of another life could not have been so prominently before their minds, and so warmly in their hearts, without inducing them to be much exercised with the interesting question, whether they should meet and recognise their friends there, and renew again the affections of earth. Especially would their belief in the resurrection of the body naturally lead them to this inquiry. That they did think of it, believe in it, and console themselves with it in bereavement and sorrow at the death of their friends, is evident from several considerations to which we will now attend.

I. The pious care and affection with which the Jews treated the bodies of their beloved dead, points us strongly to their belief in perpetuated love and final reunion in heaven.

If they did not expect to follow the departed through the grave — if they did not believe that their bodies should be revived again, and be returned to their embraces inhabited by the souls of their friends, why did they preserve, like a precious treasure, with such devout affection, their lifeless bodies? Look, for instance, at the tender and affecting appeal of Abraham to the sons of Heth, after the death of Sarah his wife, for the field and cave of Machpelah in the land in which he sojourned, as a burying-place for his dead. They offered to him "the choice of their sepulchres," but he politely, yet decidedly, declined. He wished to purchase the field with money "for a possession" — he wished to have it "made sure for a burying-place." He desired a place as *his own*, which he might consecrate as a place of repose for his dead in all coming time. His soul shuddered at the thought of committing such a treasure as the remains of his departed wife to the sepulchres of Heth, where he could not himself exercise a devout watch over them. Amid the green and rural scenes of Machpelah — for "all the trees that were in the field, and in all the borders round about, were made sure" — he would have her body to rest, in token of his belief that she still lived in the ever-green bowers of Paradise; that he still stood in living communion with her; and that he expected to see her again in that world where death is unknown. He desired that the glorious renovation which each returning spring-time effected, amid the rural scenes of Machpelah, might be to him a sweet pledge of that new and eternal life which should once awake from her tomb, and an earnest of the revival of those affectionate ties which had been but temporarily sundered by death.

The conduct of the pious and mourning Patriarch, in this whole transaction, is very significant when carefully studied. There were the "choice sepulchres of the Hittites offered to him, in which to bury his beloved Sarah; but how, in that case, could he have been assured that her bones would lie till the final day in peace? As once in Egypt another king arose which knew not Joseph, who did evil to Israel; so, in the land of the Hittites, another generation would soon arise, who would not know Abraham, and would show no respect for his dead. How too, if he buried in their sepulchres, could he be assured that he would be permitted one day to lie by her side in death? Above all, how could he then visit her grave in quiet, as Mary did the grave of her Lord, undisturbed and unseen by the cold world, to shed the silent tear of affection to her memory, and refresh his sorrowing heart with the hope of speedy reunion in heaven? No wonder that he insisted on having it as his own: — "For as much money as it is worth ye shall give it me, for a possession of a burying-place among you."

This is but an instance of the general tenderness and affection which the Jews in all ages manifested towards the remains of their kindred dead. That the same feeling was sacredly cherished among the Jews in later ages is evident from a beautiful passage in Ecclesiasticus, an apocryphal book written about three hundred years before Christ. Chap. xxxviii. 16. "My son, let tears fall down over the dead, and begin to lament, as if thou hadst suffered great harm thyself; and then cover his body according to the custom, and neglect not his burial." For another beautiful exhibition of this feeling, read Tobit i. 17—21; ii. 1—9. The same may also be seen from the well-known customs of embalming their bodies, and of giving them decent and respectable burial. It certainly speaks strongly of their belief that the dead were still theirs; that the tie was not finally and for ever broken; and that the grave, which they watched and watered with the tears of continued affection, would yet yield back to them their beloved dead.

II. The strong desire, which reigned in the hearts

of the Old Testament saints, to be buried together with their kindred in the same place, is also a proof that they believed in a perpetuated union with their friends through death in a future life.

They had lived together in life; they wished to lie together in death; to rise together in the resurrection, and to dwell together in everlasting habitations. How significant and affecting is the dying request of Jacob! "And the time drew nigh that Israel must die: and he called his son Joseph, and said unto him, If now I have found grace in thy sight, put, I pray thee, thy hand under my thigh and deal kindly and truly with me; bury me not, I pray thee, in Egypt: but I will lie with my fathers, and thou shalt carry me out of Egypt, and bury me in their burying place."* Afterwards he made the same request of all his sons, standing together around his dying couch: "And when Jacob made an end of commanding his sons, he gathered up his feet into the bed, and yielded up the ghost, and was gathered unto his people."†

What a moving scene! Are you a painter — can you throw it upon canvass? Are you a poet — can you describe it? Have you refined Christian sensibilities — can you feel it? Can you think that the dying Patriarch, thus commending his body to the care of his sons under the solemnity of an oath, and desiring so affectingly to be buried with his fathers, believed this to be an eternal separation from them? No. He felt that their communion was unbroken, and he wished that their bodies might sleep side by side, so that when their souls and bodies should be reunited,

* Gen. xlvii. 29, 30. † Gen. xlix. 33.

they might be "raised up together," with their Redeemer in the air, "and so be ever with the Lord."

The same feeling had reigned in the heart of pious Abraham, the father of the faithful. He had this in his mind when he purchased Machpelah. He did not need so large a piece of ground for Sarah alone. He wished that field to become the family burial-place for his posterity in time to come, that all who proceeded from his loins might lie around him in the peaceful arms of death, and awake with him in the resurrection morn. In this he succeeded. When he himself died, it is particularly mentioned that he was buried in the same place. "His sons Isaac and Ishmael buried him in the cave of Machpelah, in the field of Ephron, the son of Zohar the Hittite, which is before Mamre; the field which Abraham purchased of the sons of Heth: there was Abraham buried, and Sarah his wife."*

In this same spot Jacob was afterwards buried by his own earnest request, together with many other members of the Patriarchal families. Listen! "I am to be gathered to my people," says dying Israel; "bury me with my fathers in the cave that is in the field of Machpelah, which is before Mamre, in the land of Canaan, which Abraham bought with the field of Ephron the Hittite, for a possession of a burying-place." How particularly he describes it, that they may not be mistaken as to the spot! Then how affectingly, in the next verse, he gives the reason why he desires to lie in that place! "There they buried Abraham and Sarah his wife; there they buried Isaac and Rebekah his wife; and there I buried Leah!"† What

* Gen. xxiv. 9, 10. † Gen. lxix. 29, 31.

a touching request — what a moving reason! Why this desire which they felt, and which all more or less feel, of being buried with parents, grand-parents, wives, brothers, sisters, and near kindred, if it does not indicate the belief that there is also a fellowship among the dead? that if we follow the leadings of these instinctive emotions of nature, they will bring us again to those whom death has hid, but not taken away from us?

What lovely associations are these which cluster around the sacred shades of Machpelah! The future history of this burying-place of kindred seems strikingly to shadow forth the eternal union of its silent sleepers. It is stated by Josephus, fifty years after Christ, that in his day this place was still in good repair—that the posterity of Abraham erected splendid sepulchres there, which were, when he wrote, still to be seen. Mention is also made of this place by Eusebius and Jerome, and also by other church fathers, down as late as the eighth century. Even at this day the sepulchres of the Patriarchs are shown to the pilgrims in the Holy Land, by the monks on Hebron; and so well do all the circumstances agree with Scripture notices, that travellers, the most intelligent, see no reason to doubt that the tombs they behold are those of the Patriarchs who were buried in Machpelah over four thousand years ago. "I know nothing," says the learned Dr. Robinson, who visited the place in 1838, "that should lead us to question the correctness of the tradition, which regards this as the place of sepulchre of Abraham and the other Patriarchs, as recorded in the book of Genesis. On the contrary, there is much to strengthen it."

Where are now the "choice sepulchres" of the Hittites? Alas! there is no trace of them to be seen. The memory of the wicked shall rot; there lingers no living savor of hope around the place where they lie. Not so with Abraham's field and the cave in it; they are still before Hebron as they were in the morning of the world; and the pious pilgrim may still stand beside the sacred patriarchal tombs, in silent and reverential wonder, while his heart exclaims—

How many, many memories
Sweep o'er my spirit now!

Say, what means this fellowship of the dead? Shall their sleeping dust be drawn to one place by their love for each other, and remain thus undivided for ages? and shall their spirits, by whose affectionate care and desire this union of dust with dust was effected, be now and for ever separate from each other, and revive no more their former love? Who can believe it? What we see on earth of the history of their bodies is a true prophecy of the history of their spirits in heaven. They believed that their spirits would still be in each other's society above, which led them to desire that their bodies, under the promise of a blessed resurrection, should sleep the short intervening night together till the dawn of that eternal day, when not only the kindred of the patriarchs, but the saints of all ages and nations, "shall come from the east and west, and shall sit down with Abraham, and Isaac, and Jacob, in the kingdom of heaven."

This affection for kindred, which manifested itself

thus in life and in death, was not wholly instinctive; it was encouraged and cultivated by their religion. The Jewish religion was a family religion — the Christian religion is the same; it places our kindred nearest to us. It respected and used the ties of kindred in extending the covenant and its blessings to whole families in their character as families. It sanctified and perfected family love. This would naturally encourage them to hope that these ties should live, and remain in delightful force beyond this life, and be resumed in the recognition of the heavenly state. If then this, and the future life, are related to each other as seeding and harvest, we may safely take this custom of burying together, as indicating their belief in the perpetuation of earthly ties through the dissolution of the tomb.

This desire to be buried by the side of those we love is not a dark morbid superstition, which passes away before enlightened and refined Christian feeling. It is as strong in Christian hearts as it was in Jewish—and strongest of all with those whom piety itself has taught to love their friends more than they could, or would, otherwise have done. We all more or less feel its power. The family burial-ground has associations even to us, which make the idea of death less dreary; and there is, perhaps, no one to be found, who, if he can have his choice, would not rather lie at last in the silent circle of his kindred, than to be buried among strangers in a distant land. Amid the loneliness which steals over the spirit at the approach of death, comes also the desire, so plaintively expressed by Jacob: — "I will lie with my fathers — bury me in their burying-place!"

There is a beautiful instance of this, beautifully related by Mrs. Sigourney, of a little girl, who expressed a desire that she might lie with her mother, of which she would not be denied.

> There was a shaded chamber,
>   A silent, watching band;
> On a low couch a suffering child
>   Who grasped her mother's hand.
>
> She told her faith in Jesus—
>   Her simple prayer was said,
> And now that darkened vale she trod
>   Which leadeth to the dead.
>
> Red fever scorched her bosom—
>   Frost chilled the vital flame,
> And her sweet brow was troubled,
>   As anguish smote her frame.
>
> Yet 'mid the gasp and struggle,
>   With shuddering lips she cried,
> "O mother, dearest mother,
>   Bury me by your side!"

She was then asked in what place she would lie—whether in the "shady dell," where the early violets bloom, or in the "ancient church-yard," among the "white marble monuments." But all ideas of place faded before the one all-absorbing idea: "Bury me by your side."

> One only wish she uttered,
>   While life was ebbing fast,—
> "Sleep by my side, dear mother,
>   And rise with me at last."

9

Thus she persisted—and the nearer she drew to her end, the more ardent became this dying wish. It was the last request that trembled upon her tongue!

> Look! Look!—the thin lip quivers,
> The blue eyes open wide,
> And what a hollow whisper steals,—
> "BURY ME BY YOUR SIDE!"

How natural do we feel this to be? It is nothing else but the consciousness of a continued fellowship, which shrinks back with deep instinctive dread at the thought of final separation. It is the spirit, uttering its protest,—declaring that the dissolution of the body shall not affect the ties of the soul; and, on the other hand, it is the final protest of the body, asking that its interest in this eternal fellowship may not be forgotten—and that, in the mean time, it may be permitted to mingle with its kindred dust.

III. That the Jews expected to meet and know each other in the heavenly world, is also evident from the manner in which they usually spake of the death of their friends—that they were "gathered to their fathers," or "gathered to their people."

"Then Abraham gave up the ghost, and died in a good old age, an old man, and full of years, and was gathered to his people." The language is exceedingly beautiful, tender, and consoling, and points to this precious faith. It cannot mean that his *body* was gathered to his forefathers, for some of them lived and died in Ur of the Chaldees; Terah, his father, died in Haran, (Gen. xi. 32,) and was no doubt buried there. Abraham himself, as we have seen, was buried in

Machpelah in Canaan, and Sarah his wife was the first of the sacred families buried there; for he only purchased it at her death. Gen. xxiii. 19. Neither can the expression, "gathered to his people," be intended to express, in general, the idea that he was gathered with the dead; for the language is particular, that he was gathered to *his* people. That it cannot mean simply that he was laid in the grave with the rest of the dead, is also evident, from the fact that *after* it is said he was gathered to his people, it is added, in the next verse: "and his sons Isaac and Ishmael buried him in the cave of Machpelah." Hence he was gathered to his people *before* he was laid in the grave with the dead in general. It must then be regarded as its natural meaning, that *after* he died, and *before* he was buried, his soul was gathered to his people, who had departed this life before him, and who were now in that "city which hath foundations," in that "better and heavenly country," for which they all "looked," while they "confessed themselves pilgrims and strangers on the earth." Among these was his own Sarah!

"And Isaac gave up the ghost and died, and was gathered unto his people, being old and full of days; and his sons Esau and Jacob buried him." Here again he was gathered to *his* people. In this, and also in the former passage, it is most natural and correct to take the personal "*his*" or *he*, as meaning the soul, the highest and best part of his nature. We are told what was done with his body — they buried that — but *he*, that is, his spirit, which properly constitutes himself — which was the centre and substance of his personality — that was gathered to his people. Moreover,

could it be said, in any true sense, that those bodies, now turned to ashes in the tomb, constituted "his people?" May not their spirits in heaven be so called, with tenfold more propriety. He, then, — the living, thinking, loving spirit of Isaac, — was gathered to his people, who were living, thinking, loving spirits in heaven.

When the brethren of Joseph brought his bloody coat to their father Jacob, and told him that "an evil beast had devoured him," "he refused to be comforted: and he said, For I will go down into the grave unto my son mourning." Gen. xxxvii. 35. The word grave (sheol) means here, not the place of burial, but the place of departed spirits — eternity. To this place the mourning patriarch expected to go "unto his son." It does not mean that he would mourn there, but mourning would hasten him to that place, and that he would mourn all the way until he came to him. His son had gone, and he would now go on his pilgrim way in distress, until he found him in the place of departed spirits, when he himself should die. That this is his meaning is evident, for "all his sons and his daughters rose up to comfort him; but he refused to be comforted." He had loved Joseph, and had now lost sight of him, and would now mourn till he found him again: He will hear of no comfort which earth can offer. This is his resolution: "I will go down into the grave unto my son;" then will I be comforted, when he whom I have lost is restored to me, and I to him. "Thus his father wept for him."

That Jacob did not look for comfort merely in death, and by going into the grave to his son, is evident from the fact that he believed him to have been torn by wild beasts, and expected that if there was anything of him left, it was but a few scattered fragments of his torn body. He could not expect, then, in any sense that had reference to his body merely, to go down "unto his son." He would mourn, not till he was laid by his side in death; for that, in the nature of the case, could never be; but till his spirit met and embraced again his beloved Joseph, in those regions of immortal life, where misfortune and death could no more rush in between them.

"And when Jacob had made an end of commanding his sons, he gathered up his feet into the bed, and yielded up the ghost, and was gathered unto his people." Gen. xlix. 33. That this has not reference to the patriarch's body being entombed with his people, is evident from the fact that he was not buried till forty days after his death. How then could it be said that he was gathered to his people when he died, if by this expression we understand merely his burial by their side? He had said just a little before (verse 29) to his sons: "I am about to be gathered unto my people: bury me with my fathers." If now, "to be gathered to his people," is equivalent to being buried with them in the grave, these words of Jacob, just quoted, would be a tautological absurdity; thus: I am about to be buried with my people: bury me with my fathers. Who would charge the good patriarch with uttering such meaningless words when just about to die? Surely there ought to be a better reason for doing so, than just to clear out of the Bible so precious and consoling a doctrine as the heavenly recognition.

No. Abraham was in heaven, Isaac was there, and now Jacob is about to be gathered to them; and after them shall come many more, who shall come from the east and west, and shall sit down with them in the heavenly kingdom. Age after age the church in heaven has received accessions, as the saints were gathered home; and this glorious process will still continue till the last blood-washed spirit has gone through the gates of death into Abraham's bosom; then the hosts of the ransomed will be "a great multitude which no man can number."

When God sent Moses up into Mount Nebo, he said to him, "Get thee up and die in the mount whither thou goest up, and be gathered unto thy people, as Aaron, thy brother, died in Mount Hor, and was gathered unto his people." Deut. xxxii. 50. How can this mean that Moses should be buried with his forefathers, when it is afterwards said that "he was buried in a valley in the land of Moab, over against Beth-peor: but *no man knoweth of his sepulchre* unto this day." Deut. xxxiv. 6.

From all these considerations, we think, it must be evident to all, that the expression "gathered to their people," meant, among the Jews, more than being buried with them, and also more than passing into the companionship of the dead in general.* It was to *their*

* Since the above was written, I have met with the following in Jahn Arch., § 203: — The Hebrews regarded life as a journey, as a pilgrimage on the face of the earth. The traveller, as they supposed, when he arrived at the end of this journey, which happened when he died, was received into the company of his ancestors, who had gone before him. Opinions of this kind, (viz., that life is a journey, that death is the end of that journey, and that, when one dies,

people among the dead, and not to all the dead in general, that they were gathered. It was their spirits, of which alone society and fellowship can properly be predicated, which were to be gathered together at death.

How could the consoling idea of heavenly recognition be better and more beautifully expressed than with the words "gathered to his people? gathered to his fathers?" These household words waken up in the heart a thousand pleasant associations of former attachments. It places departed friends in a waiting circle around the couch of the dying, so that death itself seems but as the gathering around us of the arms of our sainted friends, receiving us with holy affection's softest and most soothing embrace. With the hope of being gathered into such a society of kindred at the moment of death, and these themselves glad in the Saviour's smile, death will be sweeter an' softer than repose. There will be not a moment's loneliness between leaving our friends on earth and joining them in heaven. Oh! to die thus, with the arms of earthly and heavenly love joined beneath and around us! Can this be an hour of terror? Can this be a Jordan of chafing waves and chilling storms? No. Rather it is like going home.

How blest the righteous when he dies!
  When sinks a weary soul to rest,
How mildly beam the closing eyes,
  How gently heaves the expiring breast!

---

he mingles with the hosts who have gone before,) are the origin and ground of such phrases as the following: to be gathered to one's people: to go to one's fathers. This *visiting of the fathers* has reference to the immortal part, and is clearly distinguished from the mere burial of the body.

So fades a summer cloud away,
  So sinks the gale when storms are o'er,
So gently shuts the eye of day,
  So dies a wave along the shore!

IV. An argument in favour of the eternal reunion of friends in heaven, may be drawn from the examples of pure disinterested friendship recorded in the Old Testament. Although we are not able to form from these a direct proof, or deduce a logical and demonstrative conclusion, yet, in contemplating them, we are so impressed with a sense of the eternal nature of true friendship, that we must *feel* these ties to be indissoluble, even though we cannot, from this source alone, *know* them to be such. We may, nevertheless, feel the highest degree of assurance that those, who loved with such pure and fervent affection, did not believe that death would break these ties and separate them for ever.

What can be more beautiful and tender than the revival of old kindred feelings and affections at the time when Joseph made himself known to his brethren? Though, on account of their previous unhappy division, their feelings must have been somewhat estranged and alienated, still, latent but not dried up, in their hearts lay the quiet fountains of holy brotherly love, which was ready to flow into streams, and mingle into one, at the touch of a word. Oh! what a moment was that, when Joseph had dismissed his attendants, and was alone with his brethren! He burst into tears before he spake a word, and "wept aloud." How must the past have rushed in upon the hearts of his brethren with all its overpowering associations, at the words:

"I am Joseph; doth my father yet live?"—"And his brethren could not answer him. And he fell upon his brother Benjamin's neck, and wept; and Benjamin wept upon his neck. Moreover, he kissed all his brethren, and wept upon them!" Such was this meeting, after so long a separation; and a separation, too, which, we should have supposed, would have gone far to root out of their hearts all remaining affection for each other. But they were brethren! The warmth of kindred love was yet latent in the heart of each; and they needed only to be brought near each other in order reciprocally to feel its power. This was all effected in a moment: Joseph said to his brethren: "Come near to me, I pray you: and they came near: and he said, I am Joseph, your brother, whom ye sold into Egypt." Though the separation of these brethren, many years before, was an unfriendly one, yet it was only on the surface; there was a deeper life of love beneath, and this was now powerfully revived. Why, we may ask, should not those who are divided by friendly death, without any occurrence to alienate their feelings, be drawn together again, in a similar manner, after death? We may, without a profane stretch of fancy, picture to ourselves many such meetings in heaven. Memory will call up the scenes of earth, social intercourse will often lead to the discovery of old acquaintances, even where recognition shall not take place at once, and there will be mutual joy, not unworthy of heaven, in such welcome discoveries.

How pure and disinterested was the love between David and Jonathan! Who can believe that it ended in death? "The soul of Jonathan was knit with the

soul of David, and Jonathan loved him as his own soul. Then Jonathan and David made a covenant, because he loved him as his own soul." Would he not then love him as *long* as he loved his own soul? As this love was based in their soul, and had nothing of the life of affinity in it, would it die with their bodies? or would it not rather last while their souls lasted? Who can believe that they walked with each other, knit in one soul through life, and then at death were suddenly separated, to know nothing of each other any more for ever? No. Friendship so pure as this, is not a mere passion or instinct of the flesh, which will expire in the grave; it is an attribute of the soul, which must live while the soul lives. Of these two friends we may say truly, what is elsewhere said of Saul and Jonathan: "Lovely and pleasant in their lives, and in their death they were not divided."

Equally affecting and significant with the above, is the affectionate attachment of Ruth to her mother-in-law, Naomi. When Naomi was about to separate from her, she "lifted up her voice and wept." When Naomi continued to urge her to return to her country, and leave her, she exclaimed, in language of almost unearthly earnestness: "Entreat me not to leave thee, or to return from following after thee: for whither thou goest I will go; and where thou lodgest I will lodge: thy people shall be my people, and thy God my God: where thou diest I will die, and there will I be buried." Ruth i. 16, 17. Certainly such affection, which knits hearts so into one through life, which makes them so cleave to each other while one after the other sinks into the grave, and which makes them so desirous of lying by each other's side in death — such love is not mortal. It must be as undying as the soul itself, in which it has its home, and as lasting as that God from whom it emanates. "God is Love:" and such pure disinterested affection as that exhibited in these instances, is the reflection of his own image in us. It is from him that we learn to love. "He that dwelleth in love, dwelleth in God, and God in him." It is His Spirit in us that raises our love to its highest perfection; and He will not teach us to cherish what must die — He will not teach us to hope for that which will lead to bitter and eternal disappointment.

Will it not be a delightful part of

"Celestial pastimes"

to revive old associations hallowed by earthly love, to recount mutual trials and triumphs, to give expression to heartfelt gratitude for favours rendered to each other in the communion of saints below, and to join in united thanksgivings unto God and the Lamb, that, under the leadings of divine grace, a perilous, crooked and eventful life has ended at last in such a happy consummation of bliss and glory? This gives a new value, and increased sacredness, to the ties of friendship on earth, and a most desirable feature to the joys of heaven.

V. The conduct of David, after the death of his child, and the source from which he drew consolation for his bereaved heart on that mournful occasion, show plainly that he believed in the doctrine of heavenly recognition. 2 Sam. xii.

David had sinned a great sin. As a salutary punishment, God determined to bereave him of his child:

"the child that is born unto thee shall surely die." This affected him deeply. He fasted, lying all night upon the earth, and humbly besought God that the child might live. The elders of his house endeavoured to raise him and soothe him, but in vain; he fasted and wept until the seventh day, when the child died. As soon as he was told that the child was dead, he changed his conduct entirely: "Then David arose from the earth, and washed, and anointed himself, and changed his apparel, and came into the house of the Lord, and worshipped: then he came to his own house; and when he required, they set bread before him, and he did eat." This conduct surprised his servants. They wondered, that as he had fasted and wept while the child was yet living, he should now rise and eat when it was dead. His answer to them is beautifully significant and satisfactory: "While the child was yet alive, I fasted, and wept; for I said, Who can tell whether God will be gracious to me, that the child may live? But now he is dead, wherefore should I fast? Can I bring him back again? *I shall go to him*, but he shall not return to me!"

In this passage the royal mourner evidently makes known the source of his consolation under this affliction. His servants wondered that he was sad no more, and expressed to him their surprise; this was his reply, in which he tells them what considerations had dried his tears. His consolation rests on two grounds.

1. His resignation to the will of God. While his child lived, there was still hope that God would be gracious to him, and grant its recovery; for which he devoutly used the proper means — fasting, penitence,

and prayer. Now, however, as the child is dead, he sees that so was God's will, and he calmly acquiesces in it. Can I bring him back against God's will? No: this he would not do. God's will is his rule; and now that he knows fully and finally that it was His will it should die, he lifts up towards God a cheerful countenance, and weeps no more.

2. The other source of his consolation is the belief that he should find his child again. This indeed would not be effected by his weeping the child back again to this world; but it would be by his following the child into a future life. "I shall go to him, but he shall not return to me." "I shall go to him!" says David. Where was the child? where did he believe it to be? Its body was not yet buried, and was therefore, so far as its body was concerned, still with him. If even its body had been buried in the grave, David knew that the dead body was not his child, but only its mortal remains. His child was in that place of which David himself frequently spake, and especially when he said of himself, as the type of Christ, "My flesh also shall rest in hope. For thou wilt not leave my soul in hell; neither wilt thou suffer thine holy one to see corruption. Thou wilt show me the path of life: in thy presence is fulness of joy; at thy right hand there are pleasures for evermore." Psalms xvi. 9–11.

With such views of immortal life, David did surely not think of his child as being just among the dead, and comfort himself with the hope that he too should soon die, and be, like it, in the grave and free from trouble. This would have been a stupid or desperate yielding to despair, instead of that cheerful resignation, which he here manifests, at the thought of going to his child. If it was the thought that he too would die, which comforted him, he would have assigned *that* as the reason of his cheerfulness. This he did not do; but he, as plainly as words can make it, declares, that he has ceased to mourn, because God's will is now manifest, and because he knows he shall go to his child. "I shall go to him."

The rich consolation which this blessed doctrine affords at such a time, none but a parent can fully know and feel. To see before us "flesh of our flesh, and bone of our bone" — to see our own image gazing affectionately upon us from the babe before us — to see our own souls and hearts beaming forth from its eyes — to hear it call us, Father! Mother! — This awakens a feeling in us that cannot die. Then, to see this image, which is but our *other self*, calm and cold in death! — then the thought of feeling the warmth of its living love no more! Does God ask any one of his children to endure this? He Himself asks: "Can a woman forget her sucking child?" No! There is a yearning after it that will not be quiet, till there is a hope of future recognition and reunion. There is no doubt many parents would have been drawn in grief after their sainted children into the grave by a cord of unrelenting grief, were it not that they drew consolation and hope from the same source from which this royal parent was comforted: "I shall go to him."

This hope subdues the keenness of grief, and brightens up the short interval of sorrow between their death and our own, and casts back the light of comfort from the distant heavens upon the bleak and dreary shores of this mortal life. The consoling thought that the parting look which we mournfully cast upon their cold faces in the coffin, is not the last one after all; and that those eyes, in which we so often saw our own image reflected, will open upon us with a purer ray, and a welcome smile, in the regions of bliss, takes away half the pangs of this sorrowful parting. This was the consolation of David; and we may, with implicit faith, cherish it as a balm for our own hearts, when bruised by fresh bereavement.

VI. Among the later Prophets, over three hundred years after David, we still find allusions, which show that the belief in future recognition was common among the sacred writers at that time.

In the 14th chapter of Isaiah there is a graphic description of the sensation produced on earth and in the regions of the dead, at the death of Nebuchadnezzar, king of Babylon. His glory is brought to the dust, and his oppressions have ceased. Now the earth rejoices, and "breaks forth in singing — yea, the fir-trees rejoice at thee, and the cedars of Lebanon, saying, since thou art laid down, no feller is come up against us." Thus was *earth* moved with joy at this event.

There is also a like sensation in the regions of the dead, to which the king has gone, at this event. "Hell* from beneath is moved for thee to meet thee at thy

---

* The word Sheol, here translated Hell, is, like the Greek Hades, a general term, meaning simply *eternity*, or the regions of the dead, without designating the particular *condition* of the dead as happy or miserable. Their actual condition must be determined by the context. In this case it means of course the place of the lost.

coming: it stirreth up the dead for thee, even all the chief ones of the earth: it hath raised up from their thrones all the kings of the nations. All they shall speak and say unto thee, art thou also become weak as we? Art thou become like one of us? Thy pomp is brought down to the grave, and the noise of thy viols: the worm is spread under thee, and the worms cover thee. How art thou fallen from heaven, O Lucifer, son of the morning! how art thou cut down to the ground, which didst weaken the nations."—The whole tenor of this passage shows that the dead *knew who he was*. They recognized him as the king of Babylon, and address him as a king. He, as a king, is represented as being received with pomp by the "chief ones of the earth" who knew him before. The other kings there are represented as still upon their thrones, and as rising up to meet him. They address him with a kind of taunting irony, reminding him that his pride and glory is departed, and that he, like them, has become weak and a fellow of worms, in the dreary regions of the dead. All this shows that there was here a mutual recognition.

This scene, it is true, is among the lost; for, although Sheol does only mean the region of the dead in general, yet here its meaning is made definite by the context, in which the character of this king is represented as wicked—he is also received by hell "from beneath," and is said to have "fallen from heaven." Its force, however, as a proof, that the prophets at this time believed in future recognition, is not weakened by this fact. For we might insist, by way of inference, that the ties which bind the wicked together cannot be stronger and more perpetual, than those which unite the saints; and if the former stretch unbroken across the grave, why not the latter? Without, however, insisting upon this inference, we may remark that we see a great deal more force in the fact, that this passage exhibits the dead in general as continuing still in the same stations, and as having the same habits, dispositions and characters, as they had here on earth. In this passage, the general features of human life, and human society, are carried over the grave, and are represented as still existing there under the same general type. Hence the dead know, and are known, recognize and are recognized, by the same marks of identity and difference, as here on earth. The whole scene in this picture is of earthly imagery, only covered over with a thin and semi-transparent veil of mystery, with which our mind naturally covers the somewhat awful abodes of the dead. Hence in the shades, or in the mysterious world of the departed, this passage still discovers the continuation of the social life of earth in its general features. Kings are still known and recognized as kings, great ones as great ones, and friends as friends.

This same view of the spirit-world continued common among the Jews, and manifested itself on various occasions in the days of our Saviour. The patriarchs are spoken of as sitting in the kingdom of heaven, and others are represented as being gathered to them, and as sitting down with them. The question of the Sadducees, as to whose wife she should be, who had been the wife of seven, shows that the Jews then believed that the ties of earth would continue; for, though the Sadducees themselves did not believe in a resurrection and in another life, yet they knew that the other Jews did; and for this reason they supposed that this question would trouble them. Had the Jews not believed that knowledge of each other would exist in heaven, the Sadducees could not have supposed that this question would cause any difficulty.

All this shows most clearly that, as exhibited in these allusions, it was a common sentiment among the Jews, that society in the future life would exhibit essentially the same features as here on earth — that habits, dispositions, character and station, would there be discoverable as here — and that, consequently, all who had known each other on earth, would there be able to recognize each other by the same marks and signs which distinguished them in this world. In this sense the passage under consideration, independent of the inference alluded to, affords a strong, yea, a *conclusive* proof, that the Jews believed in a general mutual recognition of each other in a future life.

The Jews, living in the childhood of the world, when imagination and hope were stronger than reason and clear understanding, must have found this doctrine peculiarly precious and consoling. Experience and observation prove that, even now, among simple-hearted peasants, whose minds are less critical and less logical than the minds of those who live in the light of science, the memory of the departed is cherished with more tenderness and less interruption. We do not mean that they believe more, or more firmly, but that they doubt less. With what pious and implicit faith is this doctrine now held, where there is not the ability to offer one reason for it, in the peaceful tents of humble life! Around many a green country grave-yard it clusters with its blessed hopes and consolations, and is as fresh and living in the hearts of mourners as the green grass and wild flowers that grow in peace together there. There no speculative doubts arise. There faith rests, not upon reason, but upon a sweet unquestioned tradition, too innocent and too much in accordance with unsophisticated and instinctive nature, to be assailed by such as love to doubt. Their love for the dead is quite too childlike to be disturbed by thoughts either right or wrong. They love their dear departed ones with that love which believeth all things, hopeth all things, and never faileth.

This was precisely the condition of the Old Testament saints. They were children in knowledge, in thoughts, feelings, manners, hopes and affections. Hence we have such tender and moving instances of lovely grief for the dead recorded in the Bible. The family feeling was strong and sacred; and they felt that those who, year by year, dropped away from the circle of their love, were not lost but gone before. By a holy and affectionate instinct which, cultivated by revelation, grew gradually more and more into a clear faith, they felt constrained to cherish their memory in the sweet and comforting hope of reunion with them in the life everlasting.

CHAPTER VI.

Heavenly Recognition in the Teachings of Christ.

When sorrowing o'er some stone I bend,
Which covers all that was a friend,
And from his voice, his hand, his smile,
Divides me for a little while;
Thou, Saviour, seest the tears I shed,
For thou didst weep o'er Lazarus dead.

The direct object of our Saviour's mission into the world was to reveal God's will, to bring to men life and salvation, and thus to repair upon earth the ruins of the fall. Intent upon this object, he was concerned and employed, rather with men's duties upon the earth, than with their privileges in heaven. Although what he did and said was designed in the final issue to bear upon the heavenly kingdom, yet his first and immediate aim was the establishment of a kingdom upon the earth. He did not therefore speak so largely and directly of the heavenly world, no doubt because he thought it not fit unduly to crowd the future into the present. He could have said much of the glory which surrounded Him above, and which is waiting for the saints, but that was to be revealed to them more fully in its time, while as yet his great mission, and their most urgent duty, was to secure for them a clear and sure title to the heavenly blessedness.

This may account for the fact that almost all we know of heaven from the Saviour's teachings is indirect and incidental. We must therefore expect that what we shall find in His teachings on the heavenly recognition, will be in hints and allusions, rather than direct and positive. If, however, such hints and allusions are, here and there, scattered through the Gospel records, they furnish a testimony just as decisive as positive declarations. "When a doctrine is assumed as the basis of any reasoning, or appears to be casually wrought into the texture of an illustration, it is evidently supposed to be true—nay, such a use of the doctrine amounts to a positive affirmation of it; since it originates in a belief that it is too obvious, or too generally received, to require that it should be made the subject of explicit statement or formal discussion." When a traveller, for instance, in describing the country through which he has passed, alludes to capitals, churches, and ships, we know that the inhabitants of that country have a government, a religion, and a commerce, just as decidedly, as if he had directly stated it. On the same principle circumstantial evidence is often more convincing and conclusive than direct testimony.

These incidental allusions are especially strong in proof of the doctrine of heavenly recognition, when we have other grounds upon which we may reasonably hold it by way of supposition; in that case, these allusions confirm the correctness of the supposition, with a degree of certainty which admits of no hesitation. This supposition we already hold with great confidence, derived from the several considerations presented in the preceding chapters. Following thus the historical process of this doctrine, our assurance increases in strength; the stream of evidence enlarges, and acquires a more determinate force, and we are borne along freely and yet with irresistible power, to its comforting and delightful conclusion.

With these views of the nature and value of the evidence we expect to derive from the incidental testimony which falls from our Saviour's lips, we proceed to trace the history of this doctrine in His blessed and gracious teachings.

I. The doctrine of heavenly recognition is involved in, and may be inferred from, the nature of that kingdom which Christ established here on earth, and which is to continue in heaven.

"I am not come to destroy, but to fulfil." This, though spoken directly in reference to the law, is true in a deep and comprehensive sense, and may be applied to the mission of Christ in all its departments. The Saviour did not come to break and destroy human ties, but to elevate, sanctify, and perfect them. For this purpose He became Himself human, stood in human relations, and was bound by human ties. He came to establish a kingdom, making himself its centre and life, making all the laws which bind the subjects of it to Him and each other, laws of love; and making these laws *divine*, and yet permitting them at the same time to remain sweetly *human*. This kingdom on earth is the same which is once to become the kingdom of heaven; and we may therefore seek and see, even here upon the earth, the pattern and fashion of heavenly things, though it be somewhat darkly, in inci-pient or embryonic stages.

Thus, Christ formed on earth a social economy; not thereby to destroy existing ties, but to bind them more firmly and lastingly together in a higher principle, the principle of divine life, and of holy love. The bonds which are to unite the members of his kingdom are not to be bonds merely of a common interest, like those in human governments, where some individual rights and privileges are to be sacrificed for the good of the whole; but they are cords of life and love, proceeding from His own heart, and binding each to all, and all to Himself, as the members of one body — thus securing the common good by individual benefit, instead of by individual sacrifice.

Here then is a brotherhood, instead of a civil compact — a family, instead of a nation. United to him as the First Born, and Elder Brother, and to each other as children of a family; the ties of kindred were not to be destroyed, but to be sanctified in Him, and from Him extended as the ties of his eternal kingdom; so that, in this larger range, they might expand and perfect themselves, by becoming eternal. With this blessed object in view, the Saviour-king aimed at the destruction of all divisions, and the uprooting of sin as their cause. He earnestly and constantly inculcated the duty of the holiest love, and the most refined friendship, and hallowed all the ties of kindred, as well as of affection, by his own example.

It seems to me, that to a reflecting mind it must be the strongest of all proofs of perpetuated friendship in heaven, that Christ gave countenance to *particular* friendships upon earth. He allows and sanctifies them by his own example. Though He loved all men, He loved His disciples in *particular;* and even among His own disciples he seems to show a certain peculiar affection for some. Peter, James and John, seem to have been his particular favourites. They were on many occasions, his confidential witnesses. When he raised the centurion's daughter from the dead they were admitted, and no others. On the mysterious mount, where He was transfigured, these three were the only ones permitted to be the witnesses of His glory. In the garden of Gethsemane, these three were the only ones admitted into the secrets of His sufferings and sorrow. That this confidence is the mark of the most intimate friendship, the Saviour Himself declares, when he says to his disciples: "I call you not servants; for the servant *knoweth not* what his lord doeth: but I have called you friends; for all things that I have heard of my Father I have *made known* unto you." According to this, confidence is a mark of peculiar and intimate friendship; and hence, because these three were so often admitted into his secret doings, they must have been regarded by him with peculiar love. Even among these three, *one* seems still to be singled out by Him, as yet nearer than the other two. This is John, "the beloved disciple," the "disciple whom Jesus loved," the one "which also leaned on His breast at supper!" There could be no meaning in designating him, as *the* disciple whom Jesus loved, if it was not generally known and understood that He loved him peculiarly, and that he was regarded as the Saviour's favourite.

This peculiar and particular friendship was not confined to the circle of the apostles; for even among the believers in general, we find, He had his special attachments. The Scriptures designate, as the objects of his special friendship, the retired family of Bethany. Not only is this indicated by His frequently retiring to that peaceful retreat, but we are plainly told: "Now Jesus loved Martha, and her sister, and Lazarus." His peculiar intimacy with these two sisters is also seen in the fact that they sent for him in all the simplicity of the most confident love, when their brother was sick; this they did, not without having had previous assurance that they would find in Him particular sympathy. How spontaneously and freely He mingles His tears with theirs! Even the Jews took knowledge of it, and exclaimed: "Behold how He loved him!"

In what way, it is now asked, does this bear on the perpetuation of friendship and particular affection in the other world? We answer, the particular love thus manifested by Christ, proves that special affection is not improper or inconsistent in holy beings, for He was holy. His exercising such affections, and delighting in them, shows that they are *fit* to be continued in heaven. We can, moreover, not believe that He would form ties of a special kind, and thus by his example give encouragement to the formation of similar ones by his people, if they are to be broken by death. With such vanity we must not charge the Saviour, who is the same yesterday, to-day, and for ever. In his heart nothing can live for a moment, which is not to live for ever.

A still stronger feature in this testimony, is his tears

at the grave of Lazarus. "He groaned in spirit and was troubled;" and while they stood at the door of the sepulchre, "Jesus wept!" This proves that, to Him, the ties of earthly and kindred love were sacred and holy; that the breaking of them by death was an evil in itself, which demanded tears of sorrow; and that in repairing the evils of the fall, which brought death, this evil called also for reparation in the case of the saints. What can show more clearly that, though dead, Lazarus was still bound to them, and they to him? Here we see how the Saviour, by his own example, justifies our crowding with sorrowful hearts, and with undying affection, after our beloved friends, asking loudly, by the eloquence of our grief, that they may be restored to us again and we to them.

The argument for heavenly recognition, from this scene of bereavement, becomes perfect by a glance at the interview between Jesus and Martha, and the way He consoled her, on her brother's death. In deep distress she says to him, "Lord, if thou hadst been here, my brother had not died." Now, how does He console her? He does not say, Weep not, for he is happy, though you see him not, and shall see him no more. No. He intimates to her in the tenderest manner, that what has now been a source of grief, shall once again be a source of joy. "Thy brother shall rise again." This would really have been no comfort to her, while her heart was torn and bleeding from his death and separation from her, if He had not intended thereby to inform her that he should rise again, to be her brother, and if she had not so understood it. He did not tell her that He would *immediately* raise her brother, so that it was not *that* thought which was brought before her mind for comfort; she declares also that she already knew he would rise "in the resurrection at the last day." His answer shows, that He wished to assure her of the general truth, that He was Himself the resurrection — that the believing dead lived in Him, and that the believing who lived should never die: that thus, in Him, existed even now that life which is the basis of ties which death does not sever; and when he should rise at the resurrection, he would rise in Him; and that, in Him, all ties are eternally secure. It would be difficult to see why He should tell her in the way of comfort that her brother should rise again, if it was not by way of assuring her of the renewal of such ties beyond death. He would assure her that "he is not dead but sleepeth." He would tell her not to mourn hopelessly, but to temper her grief with the thought that in the case of those who are united in Him, there continues a union, through Him, unaffected by death; and that even the gloomy night of a short separation is made light in the joyous hope of an endless life.

Not only did our Saviour thus hallow and sanction special friendship by His example, but He constantly urged it upon all his followers. He enjoined it upon all to cultivate love towards each other, as a necessary preparation for the heavenly kingdom. He declares it to be the fulfilling of the law, and the crowning point of Christian perfection. How can we, and why should we, believe that a feature of Christian character such as this, will ever be obliterated? that Christianity teaches us to love our friends as we would otherwise not have been able to love them, but forbids us to believe that such love is intended to be eternal?

If particular attachments are to die at death, never to be revived again in heaven, it is strange that our adorable Saviour should manifest such a particular concern for His mother, when He hung upon the cross, as to commend her to His "beloved disciple." Strange also, that in imitation of his example, the experience of hundreds of saints in dying have found the cords of kindred love drawing tighter, even to the seeming distress of their last hours. This certainly is no sign that love is dying, but rather proclaims its strength in death, and is a final and almost unutterably strong assurance that the waters of death cannot quench it, but that it lives in peaceful and steady triumph amid the "swellings of Jordan."

This being the nature of Christ's kingdom of love on earth, such the ties formed in it, and such the friendships and affections which it begets and cultivates, we have the strongest reason to believe that these shall continue unbroken through death. To strengthen still more this belief, we must remind the reader that, according to the teachings of Christ, this kingdom is essentially the same in heaven as on earth. His kingdom is one; part on earth and part in heaven. Christ is its head and king, "of whom the whole family in heaven and earth is named." It is all but one family, one body, pervaded by one life and one love.

The saints on earth and all the dead,
But one communion make;
All join in Christ, their living head,
And in his grace partake.

He Himself is present on both sides of death. When on earth, he could call Himself "the son of man who is in heaven;" and now, being in heaven, he can say, "Lo! I am with you alway, even to the end of the world." Here time and space can make no separation: so that, whether in the church on earth or in the church in heaven, all are alike in Him; and consequently, their relations to each other are not in the least changed. The death of a friend is just as when, at a feast, one passes into another chamber into which we may in time follow him, and find him there, as we knew him before. They pass away from earth behind the veil of our mortal sight, and there live on as before. Those faces of love which beam around us like stars in the gloom of this life, grow daily fewer, and soon we too shall fade away into the morning light of a brighter heaven.

Thus star by star declines,
  Till all are passed away,
As morning high and higher shines,
  To pure and perfect day;
Nor sink those stars in empty night,
  But hide themselves in heaven's own light.

When we shall all be over, we shall live on in His eternal kingdom together, with the same attachment to Christ and each other, only purer than here; but we shall no more tremble in the cheerless prospect of separation by death: for there they die no more!

II. Not only does a view of Christ's kingdom in this world encourage and warrant us in the belief of heavenly recognition, but we learn also to believe it from what He says of heaven, as the future inheritance of the saints.

Whenever the Saviour alludes to the heavenly world, it is always a world in its social features resembling this, except that it is holy and free from all ills. We do not get the idea, in reading the representations of heaven in the Gospels, that human ties must there be set aside, or that we shall not continue to be human in all our feelings as here. In short, under the Saviour's teachings, we feel ourselves, together with all the scenery of earth, both physical and social, transferred to a pure, perfect, peaceful and eternal world, where God, angels and saints dwell together, as in a family — and this is heaven.

Such, for instance, is the case in that incomparably touching passage in Christ's farewell address to his disciples, in which he comforts them on their short separation. "In my Father's house are many mansions: if it were not so, I would have told you. I go to prepare a place for you. And if I go and prepare a place for you, I will come again and receive you to myself; that where I am, there ye may be also." Here the sad disciples are pointed to a "Father's house," containing many mansions—here is the idea of a heavenly family, the members of which have all returned from a strange land, and now live together amid all the hallowed social endearments of an eternal home. This is the PLACE which He prepares for them. This place, he says, I prepare for *you* — that is, the same place is for all of you, that *ye*, all together, may be with me where I am. They shall, therefore, be together there, together with Him, and consequently together with each other, as the children of one family in their Father's house. We may well wonder how all this can take place without a mutual recognition! Shall they be eternally together, as children in a family, and not know each other, and without the revival of their former connections on earth? How can they be with the Saviour, know Him, have intercourse with Him, and not be reminded of earth and each other? His looks, His words, His wounds, their relations to Him— all, all would restore their mutual knowledge of each other. To suppose that there would be no recognition, is to suppose that they had lost every social feature of their original nature—that they had lost and forgotten their origin, their identity, and become beings entirely new; in which case, their salvation could mean nothing to them; and they could not feel their relation to Christ to be that of those who had been redeemed by Him from the earth.

The Saviour has also set forth the heavenly enjoyments under the figure of a feast. "I say unto you, that many shall come from the east and west, and shall sit down with Abraham, and Isaac, and Jacob, in the kingdom of heaven." Matt. viii. 11. In the parallel passage in Luke xiii. 28, it is added: "and all the prophets." That this is spoken of the heavenly world, the whole context shows; for the patriarchs were already in the future life; and this meeting is put in contrast with the "outer darkness," where are heard the weepings and wailings of those that are "thrust out." Here then Abraham, Isaac, Jacob, and all the prophets, are represented, not only as sitting together, but as engaged in social intercourse as at a feast, where old and familiar friends meet, and where new acquaintances are formed. Here others are said to come from the four quarters of the earth, to sit down with these at this social feast. The passage could mean nothing, did it not mean that these patriarchs and prophets knew each other, and that those who came to sit with them knew them also, or were made acquainted with them; and, in this holy festival, introduced into their happy society. The idea of sitting and feasting together leads us naturally and irresistibly to this conclusion. Here then is recognition and heavenly acquaintance.

As in the cases upon which we have already remarked, so also in this, the most valuable testimony we receive from this passage in favour of this doctrine, is that it represents heaven as a scene of social life, analogous to that on earth—that in this celestial communion are seen all the warm and familiar social accompaniments which are associated with the intercourse of dear friends in this life. This is common to all the Saviour's allusions to the heavenly place, state and society. It is, beyond doubt, rather superstition than reverence, which leads us to think of the heavenly life as so far removed from all the affinities of human life, that we feel a sacred awe at the very thought of transferring into it any of our human ideas and feelings. The Saviour's representations and allusions, as we see, do not, in the least, encourage this cold and unearthly abstraction. The heaven, which He causes to rise before our hopes, is one with which our human ideas and feelings can most sweetly sympathize, and towards which we are drawn with warm human, though holy desires, as a home where, what is human in us, shall not be destroyed, but elevated, sanctified, and perfected. It is this feature of the Saviour's teachings, it seems to me, more than any one passage, or class of passages, that gives us encouragement and warrant to believe that we shall there meet again our friends and pious kindred, who were joined with us in Christ upon earth, and with holier affections renew and continue the social joys begun in the communion of saints below. Would this be a bliss too tame for heaven? Well may we ask—

> Is friendship then unfit for heaven? Would love—
> That holy impulse which in Jesus dwelt, and streamed
> From Him into the souls of those who touched
> His loving heart—would it pollute the place?
> If that which buds in grace, is not to bloom
> In bliss, and thou canst prove it so, say on!

This passage not only permits us to believe that we shall see and know our former friends and acquaintances, but also confirms in us the hope, so fondly cherished by us, of seeing in the heavenly world all the illustrious of earth, who lived in previous ages of the Church, and whom we have not seen in the flesh. We shall sit down at the celestial feast, with the patriarchs and prophets—with the eminent and excellent—with holy Fathers, Martyrs, and Reformers. This will be an unspeakable pleasure—this is a most animating hope! We have heard of them, we have been benefited by them; the rays of their bright and holy influence have come down to us through the living history of the Church—by faith we have sought to place around us their bright examples, as patterns for our imitation; and we have earnestly sought to be like them, as they were like Christ. What joy will it be to see them, and sit down in their society in the blessed feastings of the heavenly world. What a reverend and illustrious company will that be! What an element of heavenly felicity, to meet the great and good of all ages, and all lands, together in glory; to hear from their own lips the trials and triumphs of the Great Kingdom in their day! The heart of Socrates, at his death, bounded with joy at the thought of meeting and conversing with Orpheus, Homer, Hesiod, Palemedes, Ajax, and all others who had maintained the cause of truth and rectitude, and of exploring the wisdom of Ulysses and Sisyphus, and the hero of the siege of Troy. Should not our hearts leap into much higher raptures at the thought of meeting Abraham, Isaac, Jacob, Moses, David, Paul, John, Polycarp, Cyprian, Augustine, Aquinas, and all those who in more modern times have brightened the firmament of the Church with a galaxy, where each distinct star is lost in the blaze of all!—and then to sit with these in the eternal kingdom of Jesus Christ! Is this a low idea of heavenly felicity?

III. We find proof in favour of the doctrine of future heavenly recognition from the Saviour's representations of the final judgment.

When Peter, as the voice of the disciples, asks what their reward shall be for having left all to follow Him, the Saviour carries their minds forward to the time when He shall sit upon the throne of His glory, and says: "Verily, I say unto you, that ye which have followed me in the regeneration, when the Son of man shall sit in the throne of His glory, ye also shall sit upon twelve thrones, judging the twelve tribes of Israel."

Here He promises to the apostles a distinguished place in the heavenly kingdom, where they shall sit together as judges. As judges, sitting together for the purpose of counselling, consulting and comparing judgments, they must, in the nature of the case, know each other. A bench of judges, unknown to each other, would be a strange anomaly indeed. And shall not those who are judged know them as the apostles? In Luke xxii. 30, where the parallel passage is recorded, the description of their social condition is still more extended and familiar; there it is added, "That ye may eat and drink at my table in my kingdom."

The offices which the apostles are said to fill also plainly and necessarily involve a recognition which must extend far beyond their own circle. "Whatever may be the nature of their office, or in whatever manner it may be exercised, it must include the knowledge of *individuals*, and of their relation to the present world. In other words, the apostles must know the persons submitted to their jurisdiction to be the twelve tribes of Israel; and it is equally plain that the Israelites must, on the other hand, be aware that their judges are the twelve apostles. But if this be admitted, what should hinder the *individuals* of either party from becoming known to one another? And, in the face of such evidence, on what ground can the belief of a *general* recognition amongst friends be reasonably called in question?"*

In the 25th chapter of Matthew, the Saviour gives a graphic scene of the final judgment, when the nations shall be gathered before Him, and when He shall se-

* Kerr.

parate one from another as a shepherd divideth the sheep from the goats. The saints shall be placed on His right hand, and the sinners on the left. Then He shall say to the saints: "Come ye blessed of my Father, inherit the kingdom prepared for you from the foundation of the world." Then he gives them the reasons why they are to receive this blessed reward. "For I was an hungered, and ye gave me meat: I was thirsty, and ye gave me drink: I was a stranger, and ye took me in: naked, and ye clothed me: I was sick, and ye visited me: I was in prison, and ye came unto me." At this the saints are represented as being surprised, and they ask, "Lord, when was this?" as though they would say, We do not remember that we did this to you—thou wast not on earth when we were there—we did not at any time come into personal contact with you, for we never saw thee in the days of thy flesh. "Then shall the King answer, and say unto them: Verily I say unto you, inasmuch as ye have done it unto one of the least of THESE my brethren, ye have done it unto me." Here, then, those brethren who had been hungry, thirsty, strangers, naked, sick, and in prison, and who in this condition had shared the kind charities of those whom the Saviour is now inviting to their reward, as the blessed of their Father, are represented as standing in the company, and the adorable Saviour, as if passing His hand toward them, says ye have done it to *these*. These, then, were standing by the side of their benefactors. Did they not know them? Certainly. For the Saviour directs the attention of those about to receive their reward, to these persons, and reminds them of their charitable acts towards them while they were upon the earth, for the very purpose of showing them the reason why they are now addressed as the blessed of His Father, and why they are now invited to enter into the joys of their Lord. They could not feel the propriety of this reward — which it is the Saviour's object to make them feel — if they did not remember their earthly relations to these, in whose persons He regards himself as having been blest by them, and the remembrance of their former earthly relations could not fail to result in a recognition. There stood the poor disciple, who had received a cup of cold water, by the side of the Christian brother who had given it to him! There stood the once hungry and shivering disciple, and by his side is the one who had fed and clothed him. There is the martyr who, while in prison awaiting his end, had received the consoling visits of the brother who now stands by his side, on the right hand of the Judge — both in full view of the joys of their Lord, into which they are soon to enter in company. Oh! the reward of doing the smallest good to the very least of the saints! Oh! the joy of meeting those in heaven whom it was in our power to bless on earth! What mutual bliss is his who did good, and his who received it. In the bosom of the one is the remembrance of a kind act; and in the bosom of the other are the swellings of joyful gratitude towards a benefactor. This — oh this, is a part of heaven!

Here, again, we must remark, how at home, amid these scenes brought before us in both the above passages, are all our human ideas and sympathies. We can enter into them with all the familiarity and warmth of mind and heart, which belong to our present consciousness. We almost see the tear of gratitude in the eye of the brother blest; and the holy blushes of him who on earth sought to do his sweet charities in modest secrecy. Still humble, he will not at first recognize in himself the one who has fed the hungry, clothed the naked, visited the sick, and housed the stranger. We can almost see the whole company moved with the warm glow of human, yet holy affections and emotions.

Such are the saints in heaven, human still. Such are the scenes of heaven, enlivened with all the hallowed, familiar and endearing accompaniments of earthly life and society. Even angels, who mingle with the saints around the throne, are not devoid of human sympathies, as appears from many Bible instances of the manner of their intercourse with the saints on earth. Those angels who, in the palmy patriarchal times, stood in the shade of a tree at the door of Abraham's tent — whose "feet he washed" — who eat of his "morsel of bread" — of his "cakes on the hearth," of "butter and milk," and "calf tender and young" — these social spirits will feel at home sitting down with Abraham, Isaac, and Jacob, with all the prophets, and with us, at those holy festivities in the spacious "many mansions" of our Father's house. It is this, appearing so often and so naturally in the Saviour's representations of the heavenly kingdom, which, more than all else, assures us that we shall find that happy place and state to be a living perpetuation of the social feelings of earth, in all the human tenderness which now endears them to us.

IV. Besides the considerations now offered, there are several passages of Scripture that appear in the

Saviour's teachings, which afford proof in favour of the doctrine of heavenly recognition.

There is a passage in Luke xvi. 9, the true meaning of which has hitherto been somewhat controverted; we shall therefore not insist upon it. It is this: "Make to yourselves friends of the mammon of unrighteousness; that when ye fail, they may receive you into everlasting habitations." The meaning may be — and it is evidently the easiest, most agreeable to the context, and not against reason or other Scripture — that those who have befriended the destitute by their charities, and have thus made them their friends, shall by them be welcomed to the heavenly world.

That the eminent of the earth shall be able to recognize each other is evident from the scene of the Saviour's Transfiguration on Tabor. Matt. xvii. 1–5. "And after six days, Jesus taketh Peter, James, and John his brother, and bringeth them up into an high mountain apart, and was transfigured before them: and His face did shine as the sun, and his raiment was white as the light. And behold, there appeared unto them Moses and Elias talking with Him. Then answered Peter, and said unto Jesus, Lord, it is good for us to be here: if thou wilt, let us make here three tabernacles; one for thee, and one for Moses, and one for Elias." — Here we find Moses and Elias in company with each other, though they had lived in different periods of the world, six hundred years apart, and had consequently not seen or known each other on earth. They must therefore have become acquainted with each other in heaven. Their interview with Christ and His disciples resulted, not only in a mutual acquaintance, but, on the part of the disciples, in a peculiar affection for these two venerable representatives of the Old Testament economy, so that the disciples desired to retain them and remain in their company. "Lord, it is good to be here: if thou wilt, let us make here three tabernacles; one for thee, and one for Moses, and one for Elias." No doubt, through Christ's talk with them, the disciple found out who they were; in the same natural way acquaintances may be formed in heaven. One object in bringing the disciples and these heavenly visitors together on this glorious Tabor, was no doubt to assure the disciples of the fellowship of *all* saints in this kingdom, begun on earth and perfected in heaven. Moses, who represented the law; Elias, who represented the prophets; and the three apostles, who were the pillars of the New Testament Church, are here brought together, even in this world, to foretoken that all the saints of all these dispensations shall at last greet each other around a glorified Head and Redeemer on the heavenly Tabor. This scene, even here, is a heavenly scene; for the veil was dropped down around them, overshadowing them as with a bright cloud, enclosing all as in a holy place, and may, therefore, be viewed as a fair specimen of heavenly intercourse.

It is worthy of remark that Moses and Elias "spake of His decease which He should accomplish at Jerusalem." This seems to have been the chief object of their visit. They had been looking on, from their celestial dwelling-place, as the Saviour prosecuted His mission on earth, with intense interest; and now, in view of the solemn and trying scene at its close on the cross, they appeared, no doubt, as an embassy for the encouragement both of Jesus and His disciples — to *Him* they spake in words which are not recorded — to *them* was afforded a glimpse of their and His heavenly glory, which seems to have impressed them deeply, for it long hovered before their minds alluringly, to animate their faith. 2 Peter i. 17. Of course, whenever they thought of it, they associated with it the remembrance of these glorified visitors, and the hope of meeting them again on high. The boon of retaining these venerable worthies in those tabernacles which they so affectionately proposed to build, could not be granted them; but who can doubt that better things than that shall be theirs? — fellowship with them in a tabernacle "not made with hands in the heavens?" It is, moreover, plain that Moses and Elias knew in heaven what was transpiring on the earth, and that they took a deep interest in it. This shows that saints in heaven are able to keep up a continued acquaintance with the earth, sympathizing with those who are coming after them in all their trials and triumphs; and, when they die, are perhaps the first to welcome them at the gate of the city!

In the parable of the rich man and Lazarus (Luke xvi.), we have a scene from the other world which gives us a view of its social character, and of the social feelings of its inhabitants. It is so well known that we need not quote it. The rich man "*seeth* Abraham afar off and Lazarus in his bosom." Here then he saw and recognized both an ancient patriarch and one who lived at the same time he did on earth, whom he was wont to see as a beggar at his door. He supposes intercourse to be possible, so natural do all things in that world appear to him; and hence he asks Abraham to send Lazarus to him to administer cool water to his burning tongue. Abraham calls him "*son;*" thus recognizing him as a Hebrew; *reminds* him of the earth, and of his *mode of life there:* "Son, remember that thou in thy lifetime receivedst thy good things." He reminds him of the difference of both their situations now from what they were on the earth: "Now he is comforted, and thou art tormented." How could they thus compare their previous and present situations and conditions, without a continuation of that consciousness which necessarily implies recognition. He remembers also, and speaks of his "father's house" upon earth. He thinks of his "five brethren," and acknowledges himself as still sustaining that relation to them; for he does not say I *had,* but "I *have* five brethren." He still feels for them, and desires that Lazarus may be sent to them "that he may testify unto them, lest they also come into that place of torment."

This, it is true, is a parable; but is a parable intended to mean nothing; or, is it not rather intended to make revealed truth plainer than could be done by plain precept? That, therefore, which is its plainest meaning, is its true meaning. That it contains ornamental imagery, which must not be run too closely in the interpretation, none will deny; but if all we have gathered from it in favour of our doctrine is taken as imagery, what, we ask, is left as substance?

It is true, also, that this is a scene partly in the place of the lost; and these feelings of interest in friends are attributed to one in torment. Yet Abraham and

Lazarus, who are saints, do so enter into the whole scene, that we see the recognition to have been alike easy and natural to each. Moreover, if they know each other in hell, there is yet stronger reason to believe that they will in heaven. For not only are the saints vastly more advanced in knowledge, but the ties of friendship which bind them together are much more intimate and durable. Their faculties are clearer, their hearts holier, their affections calmer and deeper, without any of the distortions and confusions of sin; we find, therefore, a thousand-fold more reason for expecting a renewal and continuation of former affections among the saints in light.

From what has now been said concerning heavenly recognition in the teachings of the Saviour, we trust the faith of all who have followed us has been rendered more warm and implicit. We have sought our doctrine in the general tenor of that hope-inspiring life which flows from Christ and lives in His kingdom alike in earth and in heaven, warming the hearts of all who come under its power into a felt consciousness of a charity which never faileth, and leading them to hope as they could not dare to hope before. We have followed the flow of that life and immortality which was brought to light, not only *by* Him, but *in* Him, rather than any single passage, or class of passages. In other words, we have aimed by these exhibitions rather to make the reader *feel* that there will be a heavenly recognition, than to make him *know* it. It is, with Christ, as all his revelations are, not so much doctrine as life. We have therefore laboured that our hearts might teach our minds, rather than that our minds should teach our hearts. Or, scripturally, we have walked by faith more than by sight—and "faith is the substance of things hoped for, the evidence of things not seen."

We feel sure that he who stands in full sympathy with the inner life of faith — he who lives, moves, hopes and loves, in the broad flow of Christ's universal life and kingdom, can be just as sure of eternal union with all saints in Him, as he is now sure of its existence, and of his own union with Christ. He who lives only in the deep catholic life of faith need not be afraid that his deepest longings, and most ardent hopes, will die. Things must first become fragments, before they can perish. He that is one with the infinite and eternal will realize whatever he finds it in his heart to hope for; and, to such an one, says the word of truth, "According to thy faith, be it unto you."

From these considerations we feel free to encourage every one who mourns over broken ties, with the consoling words of the Saviour, which are themselves general, and may here safely be taken in their most general application: "Blessed are they that mourn: for they shall be comforted." That affection for the pious dead which is cherished by all, and most of all in the hearts of those whose souls are purest, and whose piety is deepest, seems for its full comfort, ardently to ask for the restoration of the object of its devotion, even amid the bliss of heaven. In the tame but touching language of the pious bishop Maut—

There is a void in lorn affection's heart,
  Which yearns to be supplied. On God's high will
Though it repose submissively, yet still
  Of those, who bore in its regards a part,
The cherished forms it holds, as in a chart

Depicted, hoping He may yet fulfil
Their restitution. Pardon it if ill
Lurk in that hope, Great Father! True thou art;
Thou sayest, the just shall bliss in fulness prove,
And, what thou sayest, thy bounty will provide;
And yet meseems the blissful souls above,
The sense of earth's sweet charities denied,
Might feel a craving in those realms of love,
By angel hosts and patriarchs unsupplied.

CHAPTER VII.

Heavenly Recognition among the Apostles.

Prophets, priests,
Apostles, great reformers, all that served
Messiah faithfully, like stars appear
Of fairest beam: round them gather clad
In white, the vouchers of their ministry—
The flock their care had nourished,
Fed and saved.

POLLOCK.

THERE was nothing abstract, or purely spiritualistic, in the ideas of the Apostles, in regard to another life. They regarded man in religion, as he is actually in nature, as composed of body as well as soul, and only complete in the living union of both. They believed in the resurrection of the body, and made this faith prominent in all their teachings: indeed the sum and substance of what they announced was, "Jesus and the resurrection"—Jesus the ground of the resurrection, and his people the subjects of it; in this great truth all truths centered, and from it all truth radiated. The Saviour's resurrection was, to them, the sweet and sure pledge of an endless life. To convince ourselves of this, we need only refer our minds to all those passages in which the resurrection of Christ and of the saints is spoken of.

They had seen the Saviour, after His resurrection, clothed in a body as tangible to their senses as their own — a body, which could be seen and felt. Luke xxiv They saw Him also go up into heaven with that body Acts i. They expected, therefore, after their own resurrection, to live with Him again in their own bodies; and however much these bodies might be changed in their glorification, as to their incorruptibility, honour, power, and spirituality, they did not imagine that in their general appearance they would be essentially different from what they are now. They expected, therefore, that in the future world they would retain all those marks and characteristics of individuality by which they were here distinguished and known. Just as the seed that is sown, though it seem to perish, ripens at last into new seed exactly like that which perished, so that every seed gets its own body again; so, "the body that shall be," will be like the body that now is, and will continue in a deep sense the same body.

To their conceptions, then, the future world was as tangible as this — the future life a living continuation of this — and its social condition analogous to what it is here, only more elevated, pure, and complete. The kingdom which they were labouring to extend, was one which, in their view, joined them and all saints livingly together in Christ as members in a body. This union they believed would continue through death. Hence, when they spake of their hopes, it was in plural language. *We* are saved by hope — *we* have a building of God, eternal in the heavens—*we* shall bear the image of the heavenly—*we* shall be caught up together with them in the clouds—and so *we* shall ever be with the Lord. All this shows that they thought of the heavenly kingdom as being an inheritance upon which they expected to enter, not as individuals, but as a body of brethren in Christ, already joined in the power of an endless life, and an endless love, in the church on earth.

They also believed that as soon as one was partaker of Christ's grace and life, and entered the fellowship of the saints in the church, that he was then already in present and eternal fellowship and sympathy with all the saints on earth and in heaven. They had no fears of any intervention which would interrupt or frustrate this fellowship. The church, in their minds and hearts, was not two families, one on earth and one in heaven, which they expected only finally to be united; but, in Him it was now one family, united by life-ties, which stand in no hindering affinities with time and space—"the whole family in heaven and earth." Hence the apostle says to those Hebrew Christians, who had entered the fellowship of the saints in Christ—"Ye ARE come"—not ye shall hereafter come; but now, having entered the family of Christ on earth, you are one also with those in heaven—"Ye *are* come unto Mount Zion, and unto the city of the living God, the heavenly Jerusalem, and to an innumerable company of angels, to the general assembly and Church of the First-Born, which are written in heaven, and to God the Judge of all, and to the spirits of just men made perfect, and to Jesus the Mediator of the new covenant." Heb. xii. 22–24.

Such was their idea of the future world; in such a living connection did they believe themselves to stand with it; and such was their conception of the nature of that bond which united them to Christ and to each other, in this life and in the next. We may therefore confidently expect to find, in the teachings of the apostles, some allusions by which we may discover their belief in the heavenly recognition among saints. Such allusions there are.

There is a hint on this subject in the passage, Col. i. 28. "Christ in you, the hope of glory: whom we preach, warning every man, and teaching every man in all wisdom; *that we may present every man* perfect in Christ Jesus." Here the apostle professes to feel it to be his duty, as a minister having the charge of souls, not only to warn and teach them, but also to "present" every one at last perfect in Christ to God. This presenting we must take in the same sense as that passage of the Saviour is to be taken: "those that thou gavest me I have kept, and none of them is lost." He expected to have an eye upon them, and to feel concerned for them, to the end of their life; and he would only be discharged of his responsibility to them by presenting them perfect at the judgment. In that day, then, he expected to recognize them, as those which once belonged to his charge, single them out, and lead them, as fully redeemed through his ministry, to Christ. How could this be done without knowing them?

A similar passage runs thus: "We are your rejoicing, even as ye also are ours in the day of the Lord Jesus." 2 Cor. i. 14. He reminds the saints of Corinth of the mutual help and happiness which they had enjoyed together, and assures them that this will one day be to them a source of mutual rejoicing. When will this mutual joy take place? The answer is, "in the day of the Lord Jesus"—which is evidently the day of judgment. This implies that, in that final meeting they will know each other; if not, how could they rejoice together?

The doctrine of heavenly recognition is involved in the passage: "Knowing, that he which raised up the Lord Jesus, shall raise up us also by Jesus, and shall present us with you." 2 Cor. iv. 14. From the context it is plain that the apostle refers to their persecutions at Philippi, from which he writes, and of their sufferings in consequence. He intimates to the saints at Corinth, that these troubles may even bring them to their death; but this, he would say, is not to be dreaded; for it will neither destroy nor separate them from each other, or from him; for "he which raised up the Lord Jesus shall raise up *us* also by Jesus, and shall *present* us *with you.*"

Still more conclusive on this subject is the apostle's language to the saints of Thessalonica, whom he, by his ministry, had brought into the faith and fold of Christ. "For what is our hope, or joy, or crown of rejoicing? Are not even ye in the presence of our Lord Jesus Christ at his coming? For ye are our glory and joy." 1 Thess. ii. 19, 20. There can here be no mistake as to the time when the apostle expects to have these saints as his joy and his glory; for it is expressly mentioned—"in the presence of our Lord Jesus Christ *at his coming*"—in the last judgment. That they shall then be with him is his *hope*, even though he should see them on earth no more. This is already his joy, for he is glad in the prospect of such a meeting at last. He expects this meeting to be an honour to him, though he at present suffer shame, for they are his "*crown*." He was instrumental in "turning them to righteousness," and now he knows that "in the presence of our Lord Jesus Christ at his coming," they will shine in his crown of rejoicing "as the brightness of the firmament," and "as the stars for ever and ever." He had gone forth weeping, "bearing precious seed," but then he "shall doubtless come again with rejoicing, bringing his sheaves with him." That this text ought to be taken as a proof of future recognition, is the opinion of the learned Dr. Macknight. We quote his words: "The manner in which the apostle speaks of the Thessalonians, shows that he expected to know his converts at the day of judgment. If so, we may hope to know our relations and friends then. And, as there is no reason to think that in the future life we shall lose those natural and social affections, which constitute so great a part of our present enjoyment, may we not expect that these affections, purified from every thing animal and terrestrial, will be a source of our happiness in that life likewise?"

If any thing more is necessary to show that the apostle looked forward with joy to a meeting with his converts in heaven, we may refer to the context, which joins in urging this meaning upon the passage quoted. He speaks of his absence from them, and of his great desire to see them again. "But we, brethren, being taken from you for a short time in presence, not in heart." He had a "great desire" to see their face, and "endeavoured" to come to them; "but Satan hindered him," and he was not now certain whether they should ever meet, for they were in "tribulation," "affliction and distress." Chap. iii. 3. How these would end none could tell. Perhaps they would end in death; but in that case, they looked forward still with joy to the day of the Lord's coming, when they should meet and rejoice together.

Paul, exhorting his "beloved" among the Philippians to faithfulness, says—"that I may rejoice in the day of Christ, that I have not run in vain, nor laboured in vain." Phil. ii. 16. He wishes, in the day of Christ, to meet them, so that he may "rejoice" over them, and see, in their salvation in heaven, that he has not "laboured in vain." Equally strong, in favour of the doctrine of a mutual meeting in heaven, between Paul and his converts, is the passage in 2 Thess. i. 7—"And to you, who are troubled, *rest with us*, when the Lord Jesus shall be revealed from heaven with his mighty angels." Here again he refers to the final day, and says to them in reference to it: "To them which trouble you God will give as a recompense 'tribulation;' but to you who are troubled," he will give "rest *with us*." After the storms of life, with all the wrath of their enemies, shall have harmlessly blown over them, they will all meet, and rest to gether, as vessels after a tempestuous voyage, in the haven of celestial peace.

Is it a joy too low for saints in heaven, thus to meet, know, and love? What joy on earth is so pure and sweet as to bless others, or to be blest and feel grateful for good received? How much more — how unspeakably more and purer must the joy be, which those feel in heaven, who have laboured, prayed and wept together on earth, when they are at last safely landed together in realms of endless bliss!

> Such, Christian pastor, is thy heart's delight,
>   To serve thy God, and see thy people share
> His service, led by thee: with them how bright
>   The joy to come, let holy Paul declare;
> A joy, a glory, and a crown of light,
>   Which kings might envy, and exult to wear!

The doctrine of heavenly recognition comes clearly to view in Paul's words of comfort to the Thessalonian Christians on the death of their friends. "I would not have you to be ignorant, brethren, concerning them which are asleep, that ye sorrow not, even as others which have no hope. For if we believe that Jesus died and rose again, even so them also which sleep in Jesus will God bring with him. For this we say unto you by the word of the Lord, that we which are alive and remain unto the coming of the Lord shall not prevent them which are asleep. For the Lord himself shall descend from heaven with a shout, with the voice of the archangel, and with the trump of God: and the dead in Christ shall rise first: then we which are alive and remain shall be caught up together with them in the clouds, to meet the Lord in the air: and so shall we ever be with the Lord. Wherefore comfort one another with these words." 1 Thess. iv. 13–18.

Let it be kept in mind that these are intended to be words of comfort: "Wherefore comfort one another with these words." They were written to those who sorrowed "concerning them which are asleep"—their dear friends who had died. Why did they sorrow and mourn for them? Not because they feared that they would not rise again; for they were not ignorant of the doctrine of the resurrection. This is plain from his telling them that they should not mourn for their dead as others, the heathen, "which have *no* hope"—as though he had said you *have* hope, mourn not like those who have none. Like Martha, they knew that their friends should rise in the resurrection at the last day. It is evident then, that though they believed in a resurrection just as we do, yet like we, they mourned and sorrowed on account of the absence of their dead, under a feeble faith lest they should not see them again, though they should rise from the dead. Hence we see that the apostle supposes the existence of their belief in the resurrection; he does not announce this truth to them. He teaches the order, and the results, of the resurrection, and not that there shall be one.

In comforting them, then, he goes on to show that their dead shall not only rise, but also that they shall be joined together after they have risen; for "them also which sleep in Jesus will God bring with him." Not only you, but them also. "With him"—they will be in company with Christ when he shall come to judge the world; and, seeing Him, you shall also see them which he shall bring with him. "For this we say, *we* which are alive and remain unto the coming of the Lord shall not prevent them which are asleep." Though we, who are alive, are now divided from those asleep, and would thus seem to be better off, and have an advantage over them, yet there will be none in reality, for both we and they shall be together again before we finally enter into the heavenly life. "For the Lord himself shall descend, and the dead in Christ shall rise first." Before we or Christ shall leave the earth, the dead whom you mourn shall rise. "*Then*" — when they have risen — "we which are alive and remain shall be caught up *together with them.*" "And so shall *we*" — that is, both them and we — "be ever with the Lord." Seeing, then, Christ will come thus and raise our dead, and take us "together with them," where "we shall ever be with the Lord," why should we sorrow like those who have no hope of this kind? Rather let us "comfort one another with these words."

If the apostle had not intended by these words of comfort more than merely to give them assurance that their dead should rise, he would have concluded with saying, 'so you see your dead shall rise,' instead of saying as he does, "so shall *we* ever be with the Lord." Then, too, he would have ended with the words, "the dead in Christ shall rise first;" but, instead of this, he *follows* those who sleep in Jesus *after* they have risen— thus, "*then*"— after they have risen — "we which are alive and remain shall be caught *up together* with him in the clouds, to meet the Lord in the air." Then he ends the whole with the sweet inference which contains exactly the consolation they needed — "and so shall *we* be ever with the Lord." They ask not by their present tears, shall our dead rise? this they already knew; but shall we see them, and be with them again, after they have risen? To this question the apostle's concluding inference is the direct and satisfactory answer: "So shall *we* be ever with the Lord. Wherefore comfort one another with *these* words." So clearly and conclusively does this consolatory passage teach the doctrine of heavenly recognition.

The apostle John, when rapt in holy vision on the Isle of Patmos, "looked, and behold, a door was opened into heaven." He saw things, in that glance into the future life, which warrant us abundantly to infer the truth of the doctrine of heavenly recognition. Then was there a remembrance of the earth, for he heard them speak of the "Lamb slain" on Calvary. He sees those who "came out of great tribulation," connecting thus their present condition with their history of sorrow upon the earth. Rev. vii. 13, 14. It is remarkable in reference to our doctrine, that the elder encourages John to ask questions in regard to those whom he sees: "And one of the elders answered, saying unto me, what are these which are arrayed in white robes, and whence came they?" How naturally will it lead to recognition and acquaintance, if, when a saint of eminence and glory appears, we may feel it proper to ask, who is it? and whence came he? This John was encouraged to do — why may not we?

We find, in this vision, that the saints in heaven remember and speak of the "*kindreds*, and tongues, and people, and nations," out of which they have been redeemed. Rev. v. 9. How could this be without a perpetuation of all the faculties necessary to recognition? Remarkable, also, is the passage, Rev. vi. 9--11, which we will quote in the way of paraphrase: "And when he had opened the fifth seal, I saw under the altar the souls of them that were slain for the word of God, and for the testimony which they held." They were therefore recognized as martyrs and confessors. "And they cried with a loud voice, saying, How long, O Lord, holy and true, dost thou not judge and avenge our blood on them that dwell on the earth." Here is a recollection of earth, and a knowledge of the present condition of those who had slain these martyrs. "And white robes were given unto every one of them; and it was said unto them, that they should rest yet for a little season, until their *fellow-servants* also and *their brethren*, that should be killed as they were, should be fulfilled." This shows the continued interest which is kept up in heaven, on the part of the saints, in their brethren and fellow-servants upon the earth. We may well ask, if such acquaintance and friendly concern is kept up across the chasm of death, will it not be fully renewed, when once all are over on the eternal side?

We have reserved for the conclusion of this chapter the strong proof in favour of perpetuated friendship and heavenly recognition, derived from the nature of love, as exhibited in the teachings of the apostles.

"CHARITY NEVER FAILETH." The word charity is the same which is, in other places, translated love. Love never ends, is the meaning of it. It is here translated charity, because it has reference to that love which is directed by one person towards another, which is the proper meaning of charity. This love, between saint and saint, never fails—never ends. Much which the world calls love will of course end; because it rests on a false basis, and is not therefore really love. Some which professes to be love, rests on self-interest, and some on passion; this will pass away with the causes which produced it, like froth after the fermentation is over. Pure love, however, even between man and man, is a holy life, which has its ground in God, and its life in love to Him. If we really love a fellow-being, it is because we love God, and because God loves us and the being which we love. Any thing short of this is "of the earth earthy," and will end in death, if not sooner. That this is the true idea of love is apparent from Scripture. "Beloved, let us love one another: for *love is of God;* and *every one* that loveth is *born of God*, and knoweth God. He that loveth not, knoweth not God; for God is love. Beloved, if God so loved us, we ought also to love one another. If we love one another, *God dwelleth in* us, and *his love* is perfected *in us*. He that dwelleth in love, dwelleth in God, and God in him. Herein is our love made perfect. There is no *fear* in love; but perfect love casteth out fear: because fear hath torment. He that feareth is not made perfect in love. If a man say, I love God, and hateth his brother, he is a liar. For he that loveth not his brother, whom he hath seen, how can he love God, whom he hath not seen?" "By this we know that we love the children of God, when we love God." 1 John iv. and v.

Does this earnest sententious language mean any thing? Alas! how little is it regarded! This is the pure philosophy and theology of love, cleansed from all the vapourings of human passion. It is not built upon social convenience, upon worldly prudence, upon fashionable cast, upon external beauty, upon a fleshly, blind, sentimental sympathy, nor upon a platonic abstraction, which, like the music of the spheres, is much talked of, but which no one has ever seen.

> The law of heaven is love: and tho' its name
> Has been usurped by passion, and profan'd
> To its unholy uses through all time:
> Still the eternal principle is pure.

It has its ground in God, and its life in his love to us, and our love to Him. From this, it is evident, that no love to friends is real, except it has its foundation and source in love to Him. Love is the image of God in us, for "God is love;" so that if we dwell in love, we dwell in God, and his image dwells in us. Then we love as he loved, with an eternal affection; for his image in us can never perish. Whenever, therefore, true love binds hearts together, the same cord binds them also to God, which makes their union permanent; so that in this case they are really "partakers of the divine nature." This tie, being a divine tie, must last while God lasts — for ever! This is an union of saints with each other in the life of Christ; and because He lives they shall live, being one with him in the power of an endless life, and of an endless love. This love never ends.

Hence it is also said, "charity beareth all things — endureth all things." Lovely and appropriate in reference to this point is the song of the spouse, in the Song of Solomon viii. 6, 7. "Set me as a seal upon thine heart, as a seal upon thine arm: for love is strong as death. Many waters cannot quench love, neither can the floods drown it."

That the apostle, in saying that love never faileth, has reference to its continuation in another life, is evident from the context, where he plainly refers to the state of eternal perfection. In this world—so he argues—"we know in part, and we prophesy in part; but when that which is perfect is come, then that which is in part shall be done away." Here we are but as children, and all our faculties are imperfect; but when we become more perfect in the eternal state, we shall advance beyond our state of earthly imperfection. When we are once in heaven, and see face to face, and look no more at eternal things in the dim reflections of a dark mirror, there still "abideth" the greatest of all our graces, which is "charity." If we believe, with some, that faith and hope, having fulfilled their mission, shall then cease, charity must still continue, or it would not be *greater* than these other graces. Or if we believe, with others, that faith and hope will there also abide, then charity will also continue as the greatest of them. Thus remains

> Love the golden chain that binds
> The happy souls above.

Such is the nature of love; it is divine—the divine in us—the divine life uniting all to Christ, and each to all. It dies not. Most beautifully and truly does the poet Southey sing of the eternal nature of holy love. Most strongly does he reprove those who deny its continuance after death. We quote it the more gladly, because of the touching manner in which he makes it bear on the heavenly recognition.

> They sin who tell us love can die;
> With life all other passions fly,
> All others are but vanity.
> In heaven ambition cannot dwell;
> Nor avarice in the vaults of hell;
> Earthly these passions of the earth,
> They perish where they have their birth;
> But LOVE is indestructible.
> Its holy flame for ever burneth,
> From heaven it came, to heaven returneth;
> Too oft on earth a troubled guest,
> At times deceived, at times opprest,
> It here is tried and purified,
> Then hath in heaven its perfect rest.
> It soweth here in toil and care,
> But the harvest time of love is there.
> Oh! when a mother meets on high
> The babe she lost in infancy,
> Hath she not then, for pains and fears,
> The day of wo, the watchful night,
> For all her sorrows, all her tears,
> An over-payment of delight?

Blessed, in this land of partings and tears, is this glorious hope. Those friendly looks of love which faded from our day of joy in death, as stars fade in the light of morning, are still shining on in heaven, though we see them not, radiant in the beams of eternal love. Inspired with the consoling hope that they shall shine on us again, when, beyond the night of the grave, the morning of an eternal day shall dawn upon us, we love and praise them still — smiling through our tears! Their sanctified images hover before the eyes of our faith, as most delightful allurements. We think of them as holier, happier than we, and long to be like them. In the simplicity of childlike affection we think of them, and sing—

> Bright in that happy land
>   Beams every eye;
> Kept by a Father's hand,
>   Love cannot die.

CHAPTER VIII.

Heavenly Recognition among the Christian Fathers.

ALL the ancient and pious fathers agreed in this. St. Cyprian owns, that our parents, brethren, children, and near relations, expect us in heaven, and are solicitous for our good. St. Jerome comforts a good lady on this account, that we shall see our friends, and know them. St. Augustine endeavours to mitigate the sorrow of an Italian widow with this consideration, that she shall be restored to her husband, and behold and know him.—DR. EDWARDS.

WE reverence the early Christian Fathers as pious men, not as inspired men. We love to know their sentiments on any religious subject, because they lived in the childlike age of Christianity, and drank at the fountain-head of revealed truth as well as of sacred tradition. We introduce their testimony here by way of keeping up unbroken the historical feature of our doctrine, that we may follow it in the life and love of the Church in all ages; and thus assure ourselves that we are neither waking up an old heresy nor begetting a new one.

In speaking of the doctrine of heavenly recognition as held among the Jews, we rested an argument in its favor on the fact of their having a great desire to lie by the side of their kindred in death. The same is true of the early Christians. To bury their dead decently was considered an urgent religious duty; this their affectionate feelings towards them forbade them to neglect, and they always performed it with peculiar promptness and devotion. In the early church, the Christians often exposed themselves to the greatest danger to get the bodies of the martyrs out of the hands of their persecutors, that they might be decently buried. According to the testimony of Tertullian, collections were held in the church, which were devoted to the burial of the poor. To bury the poor and strangers, says Lactantius, is the last and greatest duty of love; and Augustine, says Stapfer, has written a whole book on the care and attention due to the dead. This was a peculiarity about them, which was so strikingly prominent as to attract the attention of Julian the Apostate; and it was even by him much admired and commended. In times of persecution they buried their dead secretly by night, because their persecutors denied to them that privilege, when they were aware of it.—See them!—affecting sight!—see them steal away, by the moon's pale light, or rays of feebler stars, bearing as sacred the lifeless but precious remains of their beloved dead! With the plaintive mourner in the Night Thoughts,—who, by persecutors, calling themselves Christians, was compelled by stealth, and in the night, to bury the body of his own daughter,—they could say

"With pious sacrilege a grave I stole."

The fact that the early Christians were prohibited from burying their dead *as a punishment*, proves that their persecutors considered this their tenderest point, and knew that in no other way could they afflict and pain them more. It seems, from this, that the desire sacredly and decently to dispose of the bodies of their dead, was their strongest passion: to this their hearts clung longest and last. For this, in the lovely spirit of Tobit of Old,* and of Old Mortality in more modern days, they were willing, if need be, to brave danger and death!

Not only did they thus safely and decently deposit the remains of their beloved dead, but they were also in the habit of frequently visiting the place where they lay; and in obscure and lonely catacombs, secretly and often by night, did they seek a kind of nearness and fellowship with them. From this custom they were often called, by their heathen contemporaries, "the light-hating people." By this daily contact and communion with the sacred and venerable remains of their ancestors, and the beloved relics of their kindred and friends, the fear of death was gradually made to give place to a strong desire to die, in order to rejoin the loved and gone before. This had, no doubt, much to do with begetting that general desire for martyrdom which caused it in early ages to be sought as a great boon. Their minds in those days of persecution turned instinctively away from the dark scenes of earthly trial and conflict, to those far-off and peaceful abodes to which their sainted friends had gone, "where the wicked cease from troubling and the weary are at rest."

The early Christians had a holy horror for the practice of burning the bodies of the dead, which was a

* Tobit i. 17–21, and ii. 1–9.

custom at the time prevailing in the Roman empire. It was, no doubt, the doctrine of the resurrection of the body, and the belief in the perpetuation of its identity in another life, where it might again be recognized and known, which inspired them with disgust for a practice which seemed to indicate the belief that hope ought in no way to cling to these lifeless remains. Their tender and hopeful affection is beautifully seen in the conduct of the congregation of Smyrna, in reference to the body of Polycarp, their bishop, after he had suffered martyrdom: "We gathered up his bones," was their affecting language, "which are more precious than gold and jewels, and deposited them in a suitable place; and God will grant us to assemble there in joy and festivity, and celebrate the birth-day of his martyrdom, in remembrance of the departed champion, and for the purpose of exciting and arming those whom the conflict is still awaiting."* Who does not admire their simple and affectionate devotion to their pastor, who had not only taught them how to live for Christ, but who was willing also for their sakes and for Christ's to seal his ministry with his blood? Can we believe, that the affection which manifested itself so tenderly for his body, did not also follow his spirit beyond the grave, in the firm hope of a blessed and eternal reunion in heaven?

It is also significant, in reference to this doctrine of heavenly recognition, as held among the early Christians, that they associated the remembrance of the dead in many ways with religious feelings, religious services and ceremonies, and with religious hopes. Accordingly,

* Neander."

their pious consciousness led them to desire the burial of their dead to be near the church. Hence it soon became customary to secure a piece of ground for a burial-place in connection with the church property, and directly around their place of worship, which was consecrated by religious solemnities as a sacred place of repose for those who slept in Jesus. This practice still continues. Here, then, the congregation of the dead was with the congregation of the living, in token of the eternal and indissoluble tie which binds together the living and the dead in one eternal fellowship in Christ.

There was, as is beautifully remarked by the late and good Neander, very early, a "Christian custom which required that the memory of departed friends should be celebrated by their relations, husbands, or wives, on the anniversary of their death, in a manner suited to the spirit of the Christian faith and the Christian hope. It was usual on this day to partake of the communion under a sense of the *inseparable fellowship with those who had died in the Lord.* A gift was laid on the altar in their name, as if they were still living members of the church."

The same which is here said to have been done by individuals was, according to the same historian, also done by communities; which shows that it was a feeling that entered deeply into the general consciousness of that age. "While individual Christians and Christian families celebrated in this manner the memories of those departed ones who were especially near to them by the ties of kindred, *whole communities* celebrated the memory of those who, without belonging to their own particular community, had died as witnesses for the Lord. The anniversary of the death of such individuals was looked upon as their birth-day to a nobler existence. Great care was bestowed in providing for their funeral obsequies, and the repose of their bodies, as the sanctified organs of holy souls, which were one day to be awakened from the dead and restored to their use under a more glorious form. On every returning anniversary of their birth-day (in the sense which has been explained) the people gathered round their graves, where the story was rehearsed of their confession and sufferings, and the communion was celebrated *in the consciousness of a continued fellowship with them*, now that they were united with Him for whom, by their sufferings, they had witnessed a good confession."

Thus with pious and lonely delight did the bereaved, in the ancient church, cherish the memory of their sainted dead, and cling with fondness to the hope of meeting them again in a better world. The apparent separation which death had caused only made them more conscious of the necessity of a deeper tie, which the grave could not break: this tie they found in their mystical union with Christ, and by all the means which are intended to strengthen this union itself, they also sought to bind themselves more closely to the dead in Christ.

The interested reader will thank us for quoting in full the beautiful testimony of Neander on this subject, in connection with a quotation from Cyprian. "As Christianity in its general influence did not tend to suppress but only to ennoble the natural feelings of man; as it opposed itself generally, as well to the *perverted education* which would crush these natural feelings, as to the unrestrained expression of them in the rude state of nature; the same was its influence also in relation to mourning for the dead. From the first, Christianity condemned the wild, and at the same time hypocritical expressions of grief with which the funeral procession was accompanied, those wailings of the women who had been hired for the occasion, (mulieres præficæ;) yet it required no stoic resignation and apathy, but mitigated and refined the anguish of sorrow, by the spirit of faith and hope, and of childlike resignation to that eternal love, which takes, in order to restore what it has taken, under a more glorious form; which separates for the moment, in order to reunite the separated in a glorified state through eternity."

When multitudes at Carthage were swept away by a desolating pestilence, Cyprian said to his church:— "We ought not to mourn for those who are delivered from the world by the call of the Lord, since we know they are not lost, but sent before us; that they have taken their leave of us in order to precede us. We may long after *them* as we do for those who have sailed on a distant voyage, but not lament them. We may not here below put on *dark* robes of mourning, when *they* above have already put on *white* robes of glory; we may not give the heathens any just occasion to accuse us of weeping for those as lost and extinct, of whom we say that *they live with God*, and of failing to prove by the witness of our hearts the faith we confess with our lips. We, who live in hope, who believe in

God, and trust that Christ has suffered for us and risen again; we, who abide in Christ, who through him and in him rise again — why do we not ourselves wish to depart out of this world? — or why do we lament for the friends who have been *separated* from us, as if they were lost?"*

Would it not increase the loveliness of our piety as well as enrich the sources of our consolations, if we, after these examples, communed more with the spirits of the dead in the element of a holy love? We feel bound, as Christians, to love all the saints among the living, and to seek their affectionate fellowship; but why, if

"Saints on earth, and all the dead,"

make but one communion in Christ — why should we not love the dead, think of them, and long after their society as we do after those who have not yet crossed that narrow flood which divides

"That heavenly land from ours?"

Yes, we should love them still. Let us endeavour to hear by faith the sweet notes of their heavenly harpings, and catch the tender gleam of their eyes, as they look toward us in deep unutterable love, till we feel heaven drawing nearer to us, and ourselves drawing nearer to it. Thus did the ancient Christians, while they sat at the graves of those they had loved in life, and still loved in death, with "childlike resignation to that eternal love which takes, in order to restore what

* Neander's Hist. of the Church, vol. i. pp. 333, 334.

it has taken under a more glorious form; which separates for a moment, in order to reunite the separated in a glorious state through eternity."

At the close of his sermon on immortality, Cyprian breaks out in a touchingly beautiful passage, directly on the subject of the heavenly recognition: I translate it from the German, as quoted by Johann Repomuk Locherer, in his History of the Christian Religion and the Church. "Precious to us will be the day that shall assign to each of us our place of abode, that shall remove us hence and release us from the snares of earth, and bring us to Paradise in the heavenly kingdom. Who, finding himself in a strange country, does not earnestly desire to return to his Fatherland? Who, about to sail in haste for his home and his friends across the sea, does not long for a friendly wind, that he may the sooner throw his arms around his beloved ones? We believe Paradise to be our Fatherland: our parents are the patriarchs; why should we not haste and fly to see our home and greet our parents? A great host of beloved friends awaits us there: a numerous and various crowd, parents, brethren, children, who are secure in a blessed immortality, and only still concerned for us, are looking with desire for our arrival. To see and embrace these — what a mutual joy will this be to us and them! What bliss, without the fear of death, to live eternally in the heavenly kingdom! How vast, and of eternal duration, is our celestial blessedness! There is the glorious choir of the apostles — there the host of joyful prophets — there the innumerable company of the martyrs, crowned on account of their victory in the conflict of suffering. There in triumph are the pure virgins. There the merciful, who have fed and blest the poor, and, according to their Lord's direction, have exchanged earthly for heavenly treasures, now receive their glorious reward. To these, dearly beloved brethren, let us hasten with strong desire, and ardently wish soon to be with them, and with Christ."

St. Ambrose, who flourished in the third century, in a funeral oration, in reference to the death of the emperor Valentinian, says: "Let us believe that Valentinian is ascended from the desert, that is to say, from this dry and unmanured (inculto) place, unto those flowery delights, *where being conjoined with his brother* (Gratian) he enjoyeth the pleasures of everlasting life."

This same St. Ambrose, in one of his epistles, comforts Faustinus on the death of his sister, thus: "Do not the carcasses* of so many half-ruined cities, and the funerals of so much land exposed under one view, admonish thee that the departure of one woman, although a holy and admirable one, should be borne with great consolation, especially seeing they are cast down and overthrown for ever; but she being taken from us *but for a time*, doth pass a better life there?"

In such like passages did the ancient Christian Fathers express their belief in the doctrine of a future recognition among the sainted dead. Such is the mellow and soothing voice of precious consolation, as it comes to us from pious bereaved hearts, over the waste of many centuries. These voices have acquired

* He seems to allude to some calamity by war, fire, flood or storm, in which countries and cities were laid desolate.

a kind of venerable authority; and we listen to them with silent reverence, as we do to the words of grey-haired wisdom. Their preservation through so many ages best shows how congenial they are to the wants and wishes of the human heart. They have gathered around them a savor and an unction, which indicates an anointing from above. They are a living and practical commentary, extending through all ages of the church, on that article of faith pronounced in deep and steady assurance by millions: "I believe in the communion of saints."

CHAPTER IX.

Heavenly Recognition among Theologians.

Like the tower of David builded for an armory, whereon there hang a thousand bucklers, all shields of mighty men.

Song of Sol., iv. 4.

In one sense the testimonies we here present have only the weight of individual or private opinion, but in another respect they are more. There is strength in the agreement of so many. These men had the same love for truth as we have, the same motives to seek it, and the same interest in it when it is found. We may therefore be fully assured that they were as earnest and sincere in seeking the truth as we can possibly be. This certainly assists us in resting, with some assurance and confidence, upon the conclusions at which they have arrived.

In looking at the belief of others on this subject, we feel also that we are not starting up a new doctrine, or pursuing a new hope. There is truth in the postulate: what is true is not new, and what is new is not true. Especially is this true in reference to doctrines in religion. We feel, however, that we are not con demned by this principle, when we find ourselves supported in this belief by the wisest and best men in all ages and in all countries. We feel in hearing them that, in a certain sense, we "hear the church." We feel convinced that an *error* could not have become so general, have lived so long, and have reigned without being questioned in so many bright and holy minds. The Holy Spirit, who leads into all truth, would not have suffered such a wide-spread and general defection from the truth.

It will be seen farther that this is not the belief of any one single sect, or of a class of sects, but that it is the voice of the Church. Men of all creeds here express their belief in this doctrine. This gives it a lovely catholic feature. It is one of those truths which utters itself from the universal Christian mind and heart. It is broad as human wants and woes. Like the hope of heaven itself, it springs up in every heart which seeks that friendly and peaceful abode.

Although what is here presented seems to be a chapter of fragments, yet we believe it will be found that the general stream of our argument flows on in living connection through it. We desire that the testimony of the early church, which we have exhibited in the preceding chapter, may come down to us through these voices in an unbroken series of witnesses — each under the influence of the spirit of truth, but no one speaking of himself. In this chapter, the reader may imagine himself entering a spacious hall, illuminated by the wisdom of ages, in which the wise and good are speaking with each other and with him on this subject; here, while relaxing and regaling himself, new ideas will start up in his mind and new comforts in his heart. This chapter is "like the tower of David builded for an armory, whereon there hang a thousand bucklers, all shields of mighty men."

SECTION I.

ARGUMENTATIVE.

I. Dr. Martin Luther.

The following extract is part of a conversation which took place between Luther, Justus Jonas, Michael Celius, and the Counts of Mansfieldt, on Wednesday evening, February 17th, 1546, at Eisleben. He died next morning, the 18th, at 3 o'clock. It is said that during that evening which preceded his death "he spake many earnest words in relation to death and the eternal world." The extract is taken from Luther's Works, vol. viii., p. 384. Jena edition, 1562.

"The same evening Dr. Luther made remarks on the question: *Whether in the future blessed and eternal assembly and church we shall know each other?* And as we anxiously desired to know his opinion, he said: How did Adam do? He had never in his life seen Eve—he lay and slept—yet, when he awoke he did not say, Whence did you come? who are you? but he said: "This is now bone of my bones, and flesh of my flesh." How did he know that this woman did not spring forth from a stone? He knew it because he was full of the Holy Spirit, and in possession of the true knowledge of God. Into this knowledge and image we will, in the future life, again be renewed in

Christ; so that we will know father, mother, and one another, on sight, better than did Adam and Eve."

II. Melancthon. Cruciger. Olevianus. Scaliger.

"Melancthon," says bishop Burgess, "a few days before his death, told Camerarius that he trusted their friendship should be cultivated and perpetuated in another world. Cruciger, another of the school of the Reformers, spoke, in his last hours, of meeting and recognition. Casper Olevianus,* a divine of Heidelberg, when his son had been summoned to see him before he should die, sent to him also the message, that 'he need not hurry: they should see one another in eternal life.' So Joseph Scaliger spoke of 'soon meeting and embracing, no longer the subjects of age and infirmity.'" How precious is this testimony, in favor of this doctrine of heavenly recognition; showing the power which the sweet social attractions of heaven exercised over these strong and earnest minds, in those stormy times! The firmament of the church rolled in tempests, but through the darkness broke this soft light from a serener world upon their souls — the more precious at such a time.

* Olevianus has the honor of sharing with Ursinus the authorship of the celebrated Heidelberg Catechism — the symbol of all the Reformed churches in all lands and languages where the Reformed faith is held.

III. Thomas Becon,

One of the English Reformers, A. D. 1550.

Phil. If your friends live in the fear of God, and depart in the Christian faith, they may be sure to come thither, where you shall be; even unto the glorious kingdom of God, where you shall both see them, know them, talk with them, and be much more joyful with them than ever you were in this world.

Chris. Some doubt of that.

Phil. Why so? Shall the knowledge of God's elect and chosen people be less in the kingdom of God than it is in this world? We, being in this corruptible body, know one another when we see not God, but with the eye of faith; and shall we not know one another after that we have put off this sinful body, and see God face to face, in the sight of whom is the knowledge of all things? We shall be like the glorious angels of heaven, who know one another; can it then come to pass that one of us may not know another? Shall we be equal with the angels in other things, and inferior unto them in knowing one another? We shall know and see Christ as He is, who is the wisdom, image, and brightness of the heavenly Father; and shall the knowledge of one another be hidden from us? We are members all of one body, and shall we not know one another?

We shall know our head, which is Christ, and shall we not know ourselves? We shall be citizens of one heavenly city, where continual light shall be, and shall we be overwhelmed with such darkness that we shall not see and know one another? They that in this world continue together in one place but for a season, know one another, and shall we, who for ever shall continue together, singing, praising, and magnifying the Lord our God, not know one another? They that are in one household, and serve one lord and master, know one another in this world, and shall not we know one another, who in the kingdom of heaven whall continually serve the Lord our God together, with one spirit and with one mind? There is a certain knowledge one of another here in the earth, even amongst the unreasonable and brute beasts, and shall our senses be so darkened in the life to come, that we being immortal, incorruptible, and like unto the angels of God, yea, seeing God face to face, shall not know one another? We shall know God as He is, and shall we not know one another? Adam, before he sinned, being in the state of innocence, knew Eve so soon as God brought her unto him, and called her by her name; and shall not we, being in heaven, where we shall be in a much more blessed and perfect state than ever Adam was in paradise, know one another? Shall our knowledge be inferior to Adam's knowledge in paradise?

When Christ was transfigured on Mount Tabor, his disciples, Peter, James, and John, did not only know Christ, but also Moses and Elias, who talked there with Christ, whom, notwithstanding, they had never seen nor known in the flesh. Whereof we may learn, that when we come to behold the glorious majesty of the great God, we shall not only know our Saviour Christ, and such as we were acquainted with in this world, but also all the elect and chosen people of God, who have been from the beginning of the world. As the holy apostle saith, ye are come to the mount Sion, and to the city of the living God, the heavenly Jerusalem, and to an innumerable company of angels, and to the general assembly and church of the first-born, which are written in heaven, and to God, the judge of all, and to the spirits of just men made perfect, and to Jesus the Mediator of the New Testament. When we are once come into that heavenly Jerusalem, we shall, without all doubt, both see and know all the holy and most blessed company of the patriarchs, prophets, apostles, and martyrs, with all others of the faithful. As we are all members of one body, whereof Jesus Christ is the Head, so shall we know one another, rejoice together, and be glad with one another.

IV. Archdeacon William Paley.

If this (Col. i. 28) be rightly interpreted, then it affords the manifest and necessary inference, that the saints in a future life will meet and be known again to one another: for how, without knowing again his converts, in their new and glorious state, could St. Paul desire or expect to present them at the last day?

V. Rev. Charles Drelincourt, Paris.

Since God intends not to destroy those gifts and abilities, which he had bestowed upon us in this life, much less shall he abolish our knowledge, which is one of the brightest beams of glory. This knowledge shall be so far from diminishing or decaying, that it shall then increase more and more, until it comes to the highest perfection. As the air loseth nothing of its twilight at break of day, when the sun riseth over our heads, but it rather loseth all obscurity and darkness which the presence of the sun draws away, until it be perfectly enlightened; likewise our understanding shall lose nothing of that light and perfection which it receives now from the breaking of the day of God's grace; but as the Sun of Righteousness riseth upon it more and more in joy and salvation, it shall perfectly lose all darkness and ignorance by degrees, until it be fully enlightened. From hence we may probably conclude, that we shall know all the persons in heaven whom we have known here on earth. For if the glorified shall remember the wicked, who have tormented them, they must needs remember all believers, who have bestowed on them their alms, and done them good.

I am, therefore, more than fully persuaded, that we shall know in heaven our parents and our friends, and generally all the persons whom we have known here below.

VI. Rev. Dr. Edwards.

It is reasonable to believe that the saints shall know that they had such and such a relation to one another when they were on earth. The father shall know that such a one was his child; the husband shall remember that such a one was his wife; the spiritual guide shall know that such belonged to his flock; and so all other relations of persons shall be renewed and known in heaven. The ground of which assertion is this, that the soul of man is of that nature that it depends not on the body and sense, and, therefore, being separated, knows all that it knew in the body. And for this reason it is not to be doubted that it arrives in the other world with the same designs and inclinations it had here. So that the delights of conversation are continued in heaven. Friends and relations are familiar and free with one another, and call to mind their former circumstances and concerns in the world, so far as they may be serviceable to advance their happiness.

VII. Dr. George Christian Knapp,

Professor of Theology in the University of Halle.

According to the representations contained in the holy scriptures, the saints will dwell together in the future world, and form, as it were, a kingdom or state of God. They will there partake of a common felicity. Their enjoyment will doubtless be very much heightened by friendship, and by their confiding intercourse with each other. We must, however, separate all earthly imperfection from our conceptions of this heavenly society. But that we shall there recognize our former friends, and shall be again associated with them, was uniformly believed by all antiquity. This idea was admitted as altogether rational, and as a consoling thought, by the most distinguished ancient philosophers. Even reason regards this as in a high degree probable; but to one who believes the holy scriptures it cannot be a matter of doubt and conjecture.

VIII. Rev. John Dick, D. D.,

Professor of Theology to the United Session Church.

It has been asked whether, in this blessed abode, the saints will know one another? One should think that the question was unnecessary, as the answer naturally presents itself to every man's mind; and it could only have occurred to some dreaming Theologian, who, in his airy speculations, has soared far beyond the sphere of reason and common sense. Who can doubt whether the saints will know one another? What reason can be given why they should not? Would it be any part of their perfection to have all their former ideas obliterated, and to meet as strangers in the other world? Would it give us a more favourable notion of the assembly in heaven, to suppose it to consist of a multitude of unknown individuals, who never hold communication with each other; or by some inexplicable restraint are prevented, amidst an intimate intercourse, from mutual discoveries? Or have they forgotten what they themselves were, so that they cannot reveal it to their associates? What would be gained by this ignorance no man can tell; but we can tell what would be lost by it. They would lose all the happiness of meeting again on the peaceful shore, those from whom they were separated by the storms of life; of seeing among the trophies of divine grace many of whom they had despaired, and for whose sakes they had gone down with sorrow to the grave; of knowing the good which they had been honoured to do, and being surrounded with the individuals who had been saved by means of their prayers, and instructions and labours. How could those whom he had been the instrument of converting and building up in the holy faith, be to the minister of the gospel a crown of joy and rejoicing in the day of the Lord, if he did not recognize them when standing at his side? The saints will be free from the turbulence of passion, but innocent affections will remain; and could they spend eternal ages without asking, Are our children here? Are our still dearer relatives here? Have our friends, with whom we took sweet counsel together, found their way to this country, to which we travelled in company till death parted us?

IX. Rev. George Burgess,

Bishop of Maine.

That it should ever have been doubted whether the inhabitants of the spiritual world recognize each other in that abode, is but an example of the wide influence of unbelief, suggesting the strangest dimness wherever the scriptures had not spoken in the most explicit words, even though the obvious reason for which the words had not been spoken was, that to speak them was needless. Why should not the departed recognize and be recognized? How can their very nature and being be so utterly changed that they should be able to exist in the same world, to remember, and to be a general assembly, a church, a society, without recognition? If the future life is the sequel and result and retribution of the present, how can recognition fail? Not a step can we proceed, not a conception can we form, not a statement of divine revelation can we clearly embrace, in our contemplations of the future life, without admitting or involving the necessity of mutual recognition as well as mutual remembrance and affection. Were Moses and Elias unknown each to the other? Did the martyrs below the altar utter the same cry, without knowing the history of their companions, each a stranger amongst strangers? Was Abraham a stranger to Lazarus, or was Lazarus seen and known by the rich man only? Could those who watch for souls render an account for them, with joy or grief, and yet not know their doom? Could Christian converts be the "glory and joy" of an apostle at the coming of the Lord, if he knew them not? Could the patriarchs be seen in the kingdom of God by none but those who should be shut out? All proceeds on the supposition of just such knowledge there as here. It is probable, indeed, that the human soul must always clothe itself with form, even in the separate state; and such a form would bear the same impress which had been given to the mortal body. There is no extravagance in the wish of Doctor Randolph to know Cowper above from his picture here, or in the same thought as expressed in the verses of Southey on the portrait of Heber.

X. Rev. William Jay.

It has been asked, shall we know each other in heaven? Suppose you should not; you may be assured of this, that nothing will be wanting to your happiness. But oh! you say, how would the thought affect me now! *There* is the babe that was torn from my bosom; how lovely then, but a cherub now! There is the friend, who was as mine own soul, with whom I took sweet counsel, and went to the house of God in company. There is the minister — whose preaching turned my feet into the path of peace — whose words were to me a well of life. There is the beloved mother, on whose knees I first laid my little hands to pray, and whose lips first taught my tongue to pronounce the name of Jesus! And are these removed from us for ever? Shall we recognize them no more? — Cease your anxieties. Can memory be annihilated? Did not Peter, James, and John know Moses and Elias? Does not the Saviour inform us that the friends, benefactors have made of the mammon of unrighteousness, shall receive them into everlasting habitations? Does not Paul tell the Thessalonians that they are his hope, and joy, and crown, at the coming of our Lord Jesus Christ?

XI. Rev. J. W. Nevin, D. D.,

Professor of Theology in the Seminary of the German Reformed Church.

That the saints in glory shall continue to know those whom they have known and loved on earth, seems to me to flow necessarily from the idea of their immortality itself; for this cannot be real, except as it includes personal identity or a continuation of the same consciousness. It is moreover a strictly catholic idea, the sense of which has been actively present to the mind of the church, through all ages, in her doctrine of the "Communion of Saints." This regards not merely Christians on earth, but also the sainted dead; according to the true word of the hymn: "The saints on earth and all the dead, but *one communion* make." But communion implies a continuity of reciprocal knowledge and affection. If death sundered absolutely the new consciousness of the believer from the old, there could be no real spiritual conjunction of this sort between the living and the departed members of Christ's body. There is a dangerous tendency in the religious world at the present time towards a false view of this relation, by which in fact the dead are taken to be so dissociated from the living, as to have no part farther in the onward movement of Christ's kingdom. But this is an error full as bad, to say the least, as the old superstition of invoking the saints and of praying for the dead. The communion of saints now noticed has regard of course to the order of things between death and the resurrection. But if we are required to believe that disembodied spirits in the middle state still retain their interest in those they have left behind them in the mortal state, how shall we question their power of recognition afterwards in the more perfect resurrection state, when those who are now in two different states, (and still in communion,) shall be all gloriously brought together again in one?

SECTION II.

ALLUSIONS IN WHICH THIS DOCTRINE IS TAKEN FOR GRANTED.

I. JOHN CALVIN.

When Calvin was near his end, Farel, his early and faithful friend, and now a venerable sage of eighty years, desired once more to see him in the flesh. Calvin dissuaded him — though he did nevertheless afterwards come from Neufchatel to Genoa, on foot, to see his friend once more, and for the last time. In his letter to Farel, in which he takes his final leave from him, as he then supposed, he says: "God bless you, best and noblest brother; and if God permits you still longer to live, forget not the tie that binds us, which will be just as agreeable to us in heaven as it has been useful to the church on earth."

II. Rev. Dr. John Tillotson.

Archbishop of Canterbury.

When we come to heaven we shall meet with all those excellent persons, those brave minds, those innocent and charitable souls, whom we have seen, and heard, and read of in the world. There we shall meet many of our dear relations and intimate friends, and perhaps with many of our enemies, to whom we shall then be perfectly reconciled, notwithstanding all the warm contests and peevish differences which we had with them in this world, even about matters of religion. For heaven is a state of perfect love and friendship.

III. Rev. Richard Baxter.

I must confess, as the experience of my own soul, that the expectation of loving my friends in heaven principally kindles my love to them on earth. If I thought that I should never know them, and consequently never love them after this life is ended, I should in reason number them with temporal things, and love them as such. But I now delight to converse with my pious friends, in a firm persuasion that I shall converse with them for ever; and I take comfort in those of them that are dead or absent, as believing I shall shortly meet them in heaven, and love them with a heavenly love that shall there be perfected.

IV. Bishop Hall.

Thou hast lost thy friend: — say, rather, thou hast parted with him. That is properly lost which is past all recovery, which we are out of hope to see any more. It is not so with this friend thou mournest for; he is but gone home a little before thee; thou art following him; you two shall meet in your Father's house, and enjoy each other more happily than you could have done here below.

V. Dr. Doddridge.

Let me be thankful for the pleasing hope that though God loves my child too well to permit it to return to me, he will ere long bring me to it. And then that endeared paternal affection, which would have been a cord to tie me to earth, and have added new pangs to my removal from it, will be as a golden chain to draw me upwards, and add one farther charm and joy even to paradise itself. Was this my desolation? this my sorrow? to part with thee for a few days, that I might receive thee for ever, (Philem., ver. 15,) and find thee what thou art? It is for no language but that of heaven, to describe the sacred joy which such a meeting must occasion.

VI. Melvill.

It is yet but a little while, and we shall be delivered from the burden and the conflict, and, with all those who have preceded us in the righteous struggle, enjoy the deep raptures of a Mediator's presence. Then re-united to the friends with whom we took sweet counsel upon earth, we shall recount our toil only to heighten our ecstacy; and call to mind the tug and the din of war, only that, with a more bounding throb, and a richer song, we may feel and celebrate the wonders of redemption.

VII. Rev. J. F. Berg, D. D.

Go where we will, we find the sentiment that friendship is perpetuated beyond the grave. It is enshrined in the heart of our common Christianity. The pure unsophisticated belief of the vast majority of the followers of Christ is in union with the yearnings of natural affection, which follows its object through the portals of the grave into the eternal world. What but this causes the Christian parent, in the dying hour, to charge his beloved children to prepare for a reunion before the throne of the Lamb? He desires to meet them there, and to rejoice with them in the victory over sin and death. The widow bending in bitter bereavement over the grave of him whom God has taken, meekly puts the cup of sorrow to her lips, with the assured confidence that the separation wrought by death is transient, and that they who sleep in Jesus shall together inherit the rest that remaineth for the people of God. Thus the wormwood and the gall are tempered by the sweet balm of hope, and heaven wins the attraction which earth has lost. Tell me, you who have seen the open tomb receive into its bosom the sacred trust committed to its keeping in hope of the first resurrection--you who have heard the sullen rumbling of the death-clods as they dropped upon the coffin-lid and told you that earth had gone back to earth, when the separation from the object of your love was realized in all the desolation of bereavement, next to the thought that ere long you should see Christ as he is and be like Him, was not that consolation the strongest which assured you that the departed one whom God had put from you into darkness, would run to meet you when you crossed the threshold of mortality, and with the holy rapture to which the redeemed alone can give utterance, lead you to the exalted Saviour, and with you bow at his feet, and cast the conqueror's crown before Him.

SECTION III.

CONSOLATORY.

I. Ulrich Zwinglius,

The Swiss Reformer.

There you may hope to see the society, the assembly, and the dwelling together, of all the holy, wise, faithful, heroic, firm, and virtuous, who have lived since the beginning of the world. There you shall see the two Adams, the saved and the Saviour. There you will see Abel, Enoch, Noah, Abraham, Isaac, Jacob, Judah, Moses, Joshua, Gideon, Samuel, Phineas, Elijah, Elisha, Isaiah, and the mother of God of whom he has prophesied. There you will see David, Hezekiah, Josiah, John the Baptist, Peter, Paul, &c. There you will see yours who have gone before you, and all your forefathers who have departed this life in the faith. In a word, no virtuous person, no holy mind, no believing soul, has lived from the beginning of the world, or shall yet live, that you shall not there meet with God.

II. Bunyan's dying words.

Weep not for me but for yourselves. I go to the Father of our Lord Jesus Christ, who will no doubt receive me, though a sinner, through the medium of our Lord Jesus Christ, where I hope we shall ere long meet, to sing the new song and remain happy for ever, in a world without end. Amen.

III. Rev. William Dodd, D. D.

This is the joy, this is the grand source of consolation under the loss of friends, — we shall meet again! They are delivered from their trial, while we are left behind a few weary years longer; and behold, the time of our departure also cometh, when we shall follow our friends, and be for ever with them and with the Lord! There shall the enraptured parents receive again their much-loved child; there shall the child, with transport, meet again those parents in joy, over whose graves, with filial duty, he dropt the affectionate tear; there shall the disconsolate widow cease her complaints; and her orphans, — orphans now no more, — shall tell the sad tale of their distress to the husband, the father; distress even pleasing to recollect, now that happiness is its result, and heaven its end! There shall the soft sympathies of endearing friendship be renewed; affectionate sisters shall congratulate each other, and faithful friends again shall mingle converse, interests, amities, and walk high in bliss with God himself.

IV. George Herbert.

My hope is that I shall shortly leave this valley of tears, and be free from all fevers and pain; and which will be a more happy condition, I shall be free from sin, and all the temptations and anxieties that attend it; and this being past, I shall dwell in the New Jerusalem; dwell there with men made perfect; dwell where these eyes shall see my Master and Saviour Jesus; and with him see my dear mother, and all my relations and friends. But I must die, or not come to that happy place.

V. Dr. Philip Doddridge.

I wonder at the weakness of our minds, that they should be so much depressed with this short separation; for these very scriptures assure us we shall meet with them again; for they and we being with the Lord, we must be with each other. What a delightful thought is this! when we run over the long catalogue of excellent friends, which we rashly say we have lost, to think, each of us, I shall be *gathered to my people;* to those whom my heart still owns under that character, with an affection which death could not cancel, nor these years of absence erase.

VI. Lavel.

Let those mourn without measure, who mourn without hope. The husbandman does not mourn, when he casts his seed into the ground. He expects to receive it again, and more. The same hope have we, respecting our friends who have died in faith. "I would not have you ignorant," says Paul, "concerning them who are asleep, that ye sorrow not as others who have no hope; for if we believe that Jesus died and rose again, even so also them who sleep in Jesus will God bring with him." He seems to say: 'Look not on the dead as lost. They are not annihilated. Indeed, they are not *dead.* They only sleep; and they sleep to wake again.' You do not lament over your children or friends, while slumbering on their beds. Consider death as a sleep from which they shall certainly awake. Even a heathen philosopher could say that he enjoyed his friends, expecting to part with them; and parted with them, expecting to see them again. And shall a heathen excel a Christian in bearing affliction with cheerfulness?

VII. Dr. Thomas Chalmers.

Tell us if Christianity does not throw a pleasing radiance around an infant's tomb? And should any parent who hears us feel softened by the remembrance of the light that twinkled a few short months under his roof, and at the end of its little period expired, we cannot think that we venture too far, when we say that he has only to persevere in the faith and in the following of the Gospel, and that very light will again shine upon him in heaven. The blossom which withered here upon its stalk, has been transplanted there to a place of endurance; and it will then gladden that eye which now weeps out the agony of an affection that has been sorely wounded; and, in the name of Him who, if on earth, would have wept along with them, do we bid all believers present to sorrow not even as others which have no hope; but to take comfort in the hope of that country where there is no sorrow and no separation.

VIII. Rev. John Newton.

I need not say to myself, or my dear friends who are in the Lord, *Quo nunc abibis in loco?* We know where they are, and how employed. There I humbly trust my dear Mary is waiting for me, and in the Lord's own time I hope to join with her and all the redeemed in praising the Lamb, once upon the cross, now upon the throne of Glory.

IX. Fenelon.

If we are sorrowing under a misfortune, of which this world affords no alleviation, the death of those most dear to us, let us humbly offer to our God the beloved whom we have lost. And what, after all, have we lost? — the remaining days of a being, whom we indeed loved, but whose happiness we do not consider in our regret; who, perhaps, was not happy here, but who certainly must be much happier with God; and whom we *shall meet again*, not in this dark and sorrowful scene, but in the bright regions of eternal day, and partake in the inexpressible happiness of eternity.

He has placed the friends whom he has taken from us in safety, to restore them to us in eternity. He has deprived us of them, that he may teach us to love them with a pure love, a love that we may enjoy in his presence for ever; he confers a greater blessing than we were capable of desiring.

Very soon they who are separated will be reunited, and there will appear no trace of the separation. They who are about to set out upon a journey, ought not to feel themselves far distant from those who have gone to the same country a few days before. Life is like a torrent; the past is but a dream; the present, while we are thinking of it, escapes us, and is precipitated into the same abyss that has swallowed up the past; the future will not be of a different nature; it will pass as rapidly. A few moments, and a few more, and all will be ended; what has appeared long and tedious, will seem short when it is finished.

X. Rev. John James, D. D.,

Prebendary of Peterborough.

It is no dreaming fancy to expect, that in *another* world we shall preserve our identity—shall know and be known even as in this. Let the mourner in Sion continue "patient in well-doing;" "looking for and hasting to the coming of the Lord," when shall begin the reunion of kindred spirits, whom in this world death had separated. Parent to child, sister to brother, husband to wife, friend to friend, shall then be restored—a blessed communion of saints, whom nor sin nor sorrow shall sever more.

XI. Rev. Thomas Smyth, D. D.

Can we not with David rejoicingly declare, 'They cannot come to us, but we can go to them?' Yes, we can go to them. "They are not lost, but gone before."

There in that world of light, and love, and joy, they await our coming. There do they beckon us to ascend. There do they stand ready to welcome us. There may we meet them, when a few more suns or seasons shall have cast their departing shadows upon our silent grave. Then shall our joy be full and our sorrows ended, and all tears wiped from our eyes.

Death separates, but it can never disunite those who are bound together in Christ Jesus. To them, death in his power of an endless separation, is abolished. It is no more death, but a sweet departure, a journey from earth to heaven. Our children are still ours. We are still their parents. We are yet one family — one in memory — one in hope — one in spirit. Our children are yet with us, and dwell with us in our sweetest, fondest recollections. We too are yet with them in the bright anticipations of our reunion with them, in the glories of the upper sanctuary. We mingle together indeed no more in sorrow and in pain,

> But we shall join love's buried ones again
> In endless bands, and in eternal peace.

XII. Rev. S. S. Schmucker, D. D.,

Professor of Theology, Gettysburg, Pennsylvania.

And how could Abraham's bosom, the region of the blessed, be other than a state of enjoyment to the Christian? There we shall see Lazarus, and be comforted with him! There we shall see father Abraham, and rest from all our sorrows, reclining on his bosom! There we shall see the ancient patriarchs and prophets!

There we shall see Jeremiah, who wept over the desolations of Israel; and Daniel, who, in defiance of the king and all his nobles, prayed three times a day to his God, and whom his God saved from the mouth of the lions! There we shall find the apostles, and Luther, and Calvin, and Zwinglius, and all that host of worthies of whom the world was not worthy, who, amid a wicked and perverse generation, maintained their fidelity to the end, and received not the mark of the beast. How can the place of departed spirits fail to be a place of joy to the Christian? for there he shall meet all those pious relatives and friends whom heaven indulgent gave to him awhile, and heaven mysterious soon resumed again.

CHAPTER X.

Heavenly Recognition among the Poets.

Poetry has been to me its own "exceeding great reward:" it has soothed my afflictions; it has multiplied and refined my enjoyments; it has endeared solitude; and it has given me the habit of wishing to discover the Good and the Beautiful in all that meets and surrounds me. COLERIDGE.

THAT is a significant and instructive fable, which the ancients record, of Orpheus the god of Poetry and Song. His wife Eurydice, according to the story, died of the bite of a serpent. Her husband was so affected by grief for her loss, that he followed her into the shades, whither her spirit had gone. As music and poetry were natural to Orpheus, he employed their powerful influence in the infernal regions with such success as to move even Pluto and Proserpine to compassion, and induced them to restore to him his beloved wife. Thus the injury which the serpent inflicted was repaired, and even death and hell were induced to let go their hold, charmed by the song of Orpheus. Is not this a prophecy of another charmer, who heals the poisonous wounds of another serpent, and turns back the captivity of death into a life everlasting? Not less significant is the end of the fable according to which Orpheus concluded his life on earth by being changed into a swan, which is the cause of its sweet notes in dying. We know of another, from whose death saints and angels have learned their sweetest song, which, like the notes of the dying swan, has lingered upon the lips of the saints in the hour of death in unearthly strains.

This is a fable, but it may show us what a powerful and soothing influence poetry and song were known to exert in all ages and among all nations. Though it will not bring our loved ones back, as did the notes of Orpheus, it may teach us whither they have gone, and encourage us to look for them again,—and this it will do, not in cold abstract logic, but in the sweet persuasive language of the heart. It may be to our hearts what the warm breath of the south is to flower-buds—it can cause them to open in love and hope towards those whose warm affections seem for a time to have retired from us into the silent mysteries of the tomb. It can soothe us, as with a soft friendly voice, while we continue to weep along life's checkered way. Who has not felt its power? The wisest and the best have crowned their wisdom with its garlands, and have sat, like children, at its feet in the quiet hours of life. Even the Bible is not ashamed of it. It hangs its heavenly colourings around the visions of the prophets, and mingles its strains with the public and private devotions of the saints.

"The great end of Poetry is to instruct, at the same time that it gives pleasure. By the decorations of elegance, and the harmony of numbers, it is well calculated to win its way both to the heart and understanding,—like a still and placid stream which beautifies and enriches all around it. Hence, from the earliest ages, when the first hymn of praise, as it were the song of the morning star, was borne on the wings of the cherubim to the throne of glory, Poetry has ever been a principal medium for communicating instruction to the mind, and captivating the affections of the heart. The truth of this remark is well illustrated by the use which all know has been made of it by the poets of the ancients, to instruct in the various arts and sciences, as well as to incite to deeds of heroism, and to lives of virtue."

The representation of this doctrine by the Poets will be useful, and we believe welcome, to our readers. In following this subject among the poets, we arrange their ideas under three heads — as argumentative — as containing incidental allusions to this subject — and as consolatory.

SECTION I.

ARGUMENTATIVE POETRY.

I.

In the first piece we introduce, the reader will find a number of forcible arguments, beautifully connected, and happily expressed. They are so much the more striking to us, because they are placed in such fair contrast with the opposing error.

RECOGNITION IN HEAVEN.

Some tell us all earthly love must die,
  Nor enter the heavenly land;
That friendship is lost above the sky
  'Midst the happy and joyous band.
And can it be so? On that blissful shore
Shall we meet the lov'd we have lost no more?

They tell us that those unseen on earth
  Shall be dear as an only child;
And the mother belov'd, who gave us birth,
  Shall be met as the savage wild!
And can it be so? in that land of love,
Are there no joys of reunion above?

They tell us the pastor, who taught us the way
  To the blessed abode of the just,
Shall know us no more in eternity's day,
  Tho' the body's redeem'd from the dust.
And can it be so, in that world of bliss?
  Shall we love less *there* than we do in *this?*

They tell us the martyr who fell on the shore,
  'Mid the war-cry, and horror untold,
Shall meet his lov'd flock with joy no more
  Than the merchant who traffics for gold.
And will it be so, in that golden street
  Where Williams, and all he held dear, shall meet?

Is *ignorance* found in the spirit's home?
  Is *memory* left in the dust?
Then shall we not feel that we stand *alone*,
  As strangers among the just?
And can it be so, in that city of light,
  Where love is unfading, and joy ever bright?

Is darkness found in that cloudless sky
  Veiling the life just pass'd:
Forgotten the friends who saw us die
  All faithful and true to the last?
And can it be so? — Shall we meet no more
When this feverish dream of life is o'er?

Then where is the pastor's "crown of joy,"
  And where the reward of the saint's employ?
And why do we cherish this restless love,
  If all will be lost or forgotten above?
Oh! can it be thus,—in that blissful place
  Where we see the redeem'd ones face to face?

II.

HEAVENLY RECOGNITION.

Oft weeping memory sits alone,
  Beside some grave at even:
And calls upon some spirit flown,
Oh say shall those on earth our own,
  Be ours again — in heaven?

Amid these lone sepulchral shades,
  Where sleep our dear ones riven,
Is not some lingering spirit near,
To tell if those divided here,
  Unite and know — in heaven?

Shall friends who o'er the waste of life,
  By the same storms are driven;
Shall they recount in realms of bliss,
The fortunes and the tears of this,
  And love again — in heaven?

When hearts, which have on earth been one,
  By ruthless death are riven:
Why does the one which death has reft
Drag off in grief the one that's left,
  If not to meet — in heaven?

The warmest love on earth is still
  Imperfect when 'tis given;
But there's a purer clime above,
Where perfect hearts in perfect love
  Unite: and this — is heaven.

If love on earth is but "in part"
  As light and shade at even:
If sin doth plant a thorn between
The truest hearts; there is, I ween
  A perfect love — in heaven

Oh happy world! Oh glorious place!
  Where all who are forgiven,
Shall find their loved and lost below,
And hearts, like meeting streams, shall flow
  For ever one — in heaven.

III.

The middle verse of the preceding poem embodies the idea, that sometimes grief for the dead has the effect of drawing the bereaved one after the one that has departed. That poem was written before the author had contemplated a volume on this subject; and also before he had seen the remarkable incident upon which the following beautiful and affecting verses are founded. This instance, as well as others which might be produced, shows that the idea above referred to is no fancy. It certainly shows a strength of affection which it is hard to consider mortal. It is, indeed, only a verification of the scripture declaration: "Love is strong as death!" Songs viii. 6.

AN INDIAN MOTHER'S LOVE.

Os-he-ouh-mai, the wife of Little Wolf, one of the Iowa Indians, died while at Paris, of an affection of the lungs, brought on by grief for the death of her young child in London. Her husband was unremitting in his endeavours to console and restore her to the love of life; but she constantly replied — "No! no! my four children recall me. I see them by the side of the Great Spirit. They stretch out their arms to me, and are astonished that I do not join them."

No! no! I must depart
From earth's pleasant scenes, for they but wake
Those thrilling memories of the lost which shake
The life-sands from my heart.

Why do ye bid me stay?
Should the rose linger when the young buds die,
Or the tree flourish when the branches lie
Stricken by sad decay?

Doth not the parent dove,
When her young nurslings leave their lowly home
And soar on joyous wings to heaven's blue dome,
Fly the deserted grove?

Why then should I remain?
Have I not seen my sweet-voiced warblers soar,
So far away that Love's fond wiles no more
May lure them back again?

They cannot come to me;
But I may go to them — and as the flower
Awaits the dewy eve, I wait the hour
That sets my spirit free.

Hark! heard ye not a sound
Sweeter than wild-bird's note or minstrel's lay?
I know that music well, for night and day
I hear it echoing round.

It is the tuneful chime
Of spirit voices! — 'tis my infant band
Calling the mourner from this darkened land
To joy's unclouded clime.

My beautiful, my blest!
I see them there, by the Great Spirit's throne;
With winning words and fond beseeching tone
They woo me to my rest.

They chide my long delay,
And wonder that I linger from their home;
They stretch their loving arms to bid me come—
Now would ye have me stay?

E. S. S.

IV.

KNOWLEDGE OF EACH OTHER IN HEAVEN.

I count the hope no day-dream of the mind,
No vision fair of transitory hue,
The souls of those, whom once on earth we knew,
And lov'd, and walk'd with in communion kind,
Departed hence, again in heaven to find.
Such hope to nature's sympathies is true;
And such, we deem, the holy word to view
Unfolds: an antidote for grief designed,
One drop from comfort's well. 'Tis true we read
The Book of life: but if we read amiss,
By God prepared fresh treasures shall succeed
To kinsmen, fellows, friends, a vast abyss
Of joy; nor aught the longing spirit need
To fill its measure of enormous bliss.

Bishop Mant.

V.

In the beautiful poem of Montgomery, this doctrine is sweetly imbedded. It is not so much the logic as the life which gives this piece such strength to win our heart. We call it beautiful, and feel its influence, without asking closely in what its strength lies. Like a real friend, it bears acquaintance, and yields more richly in proportion as it is studied. Thousands have loved it who could not tell why—a real evidence of its excellence—because it lays hold of our life deeper than that part of us which renders a reason.

NOT LOST, BUT GONE BEFORE.

Friend after friend departs;
  Who hath not lost a friend?
There is no union here of hearts,
  That finds not here an end:
Were this frail world our final rest,
Living or dying none were blest.

Beyond the flight of time,
  Beyond the reign of death,
There surely is some blessed clime,
  Where life is not a breath;
Nor life's affections transient fire,
  Whose sparks fly upward and expire.

There is a world above,
  Where parting is unknown;
A long eternity of love,
  Formed for the good alone;
And faith beholds the dying here,
  Translated to that glorious sphere.

Thus star by star declines,
  'Till all are passed away,
As morning high, and higher shines,
  To pure and perfect day;
Nor sink those stars in empty night,
  But hide themselves in heaven's own light.

SECTION II.

INCIDENTAL ALLUSIONS.

By these incidental allusions to this doctrine among the Poets, we learn not only how generally it was believed by them, but also how firmly and comfortably it sits upon the heart, especially in its silent and meditative hours. We see how naturally the heart, flowing into the griefs of others in the sweet stream of song, glides calmly on to this delightful conclusion. Most of these sentiments were expressed under a fresh sense of bereavement, and are therefore real living words. Either the Poet is comforting his own aching heart, or the heart of a friend. If it is his own, it is significant that he makes no apology and offers no argument in favour of the sentiment he utters, but firmly and in faith alludes to it as a settled truth. When it is another's sorrow he seeks to assuage, the allusion shows how naturally he takes it for granted, that the friend whom he thus incidentally reminds of this doctrine has no doubts as to its truth.

And how easily do our hearts and our convictions follow him in these allusions. He speaks *in* us, and we hear him gladly. He utters our griefs, he directs our longings, better than we could ourselves; and we are content that he should lead us on in the bright path of our hopes, to find the loved and lost again.

I.

Here is a stanza, the full tenderness of which none but a bereaved mother can feel.

> Oh! when a mother meets on high,
> The child she lost in infancy;
> Hath she not then for pains and fears,
> The day of woe, the watchful night,
> For all her sorrows, all her tears,
> An over-payment of delight?

II.

In the Sacred Lyrics of R. Huie is a beautiful poem on the death of his little son, which winds up with an allusion to this doctrine. Here is the last verse. Where is there any scripture to forbid us the hope expressed in the last line?

My little one, my fair one, thou canst not come to me,
But nearer draws the numbered hour, when I shall go to thee;
And thou, perchance, with seraph smile, and golden harp in hand,
May'st come the first to welcome me, to our Emanuel's land.

III.

Oh blissful scene! where severed hearts
  Renew the ties most cherished;
Where nought the mourned and mourner parts;
  Where grief with life is perished.
Oh! nought do I desire so well,
  As here to die, and there to dwell!

IV.

All is not over with earth's broken tie—
Where, where should sisters love, if not on high?

MRS. HEMANS.

V.

I look to recognize again, through the beautiful mask of their perfection,
The dear familiar faces I have somewhile loved on earth;
I long to talk with grateful tongue of storms and perils past,
And praise the mighty Pilot that hath steered us through the rapids.

M. F. TUPPER.

18

VI.

The saints on earth, when sweetly they converse,
And the dear favors of kind heaven rehearse,
Each feels the other's joys, both doubly share
The blessings which devoutly they compare.
If saints such mutual joy feel here below,
When they each other's heavenly foretastes know,
What joys transport them at each other's sight,
When they shall meet in empyreal height!
Friends, even in heaven, one happiness would miss,
Should they not know each other when in bliss.

BISHOP KEN.

VII.

There is only a certain class of mourners who can feel the tenderness of the following touching allusion of Southey. For them it is here inserted. As in piety, so in mourning, there is a *secret* which belongs entirely to those who have it by their own experience.

Our first-born and our only babe bereft!
Too fair a flower was she for this rude earth!
The features of her beauteous infancy
Have faded from me, like a passing cloud,
Or like the glories of an evening sky:
And seldom hath my tongue pronounced her name
Since she was summoned to a happier sphere.
But that dear love, so deeply wounded then,
I in my soul with silent faith sincere
Devoutly cherish till we meet again.

VIII.

'Tis sweet, as year by year we lose
Friends out of sight, in faith to muse
How grows in Paradise our store.

IX.

A treasure but removed—
A bright bird parted for a clearer day—
Yours still in heaven!

X.

A Mother's Lament.

I loved thee, daughter of my heart;
My child, I loved thee dearly;
And though we only met to part,—
How sweetly! how severely!—
Nor life nor death can sever
My soul from thine for ever.

Thy days, my little one, were few;
An angel's morning visit,
That came and vanished with the dew,
'Twas here,—'tis gone—where is it?
Yet didst thou leave behind thee
A clue for love to find thee.

Sarah! my last, my youngest love,
The crown of every other!
Though thou art born in heaven above,
I am thine only Mother!
Nor will affection let me
Believe thou canst forget me.

Then—thou in heaven and I on earth—
May this one hope delight us,
That thou wilt hail my second birth,
When death shall reunite us,
Where worlds no more can sever
Parent and child for ever.

Montgomery.

XI.

Departed Friends.

How natural it is, when we gaze upon the bright skies in a beautiful star-light night, to think of the spirits of the dead! This all have experienced. Then, what a feeling comes over us, strangely made up of silent dread, inward joy, and holy longing. The poem we here introduce, was written under the influence of such a night scene, and commends itself to the heart.

Who ever looked upon yon starry spheres,
  Which brightly shine from out the dark blue sky,
Nor call'd to mind the friends of other years,
The hopes, the joys, the transient smiles and tears,
  Gushing from out where buried memories lie,
  And waking the full heart to highest ecstacy!

Oh, what a glorious vision, when the moon,
  Silently gliding through her pathless way,
Has reached the extremest point of her high noon,
Shedding o'er this our earth her radiant boon,
  While twinkling stars, and orbs of steadier ray,
  Shine with a light that mocks the intenser glare of day!

Oh, who has ever gazed on such a scene,
  Nor thought the spirits of the blest were there?
Who, that beholds not in that blue serene,
Bright isles, the abode of pleasures yet unseen,
  Except by those who, freed from mortal care,
  Have winged their raptur'd flight to realms of upper air

The mother, who has watched with sleepless eye
  Her babe, and rocked with tireless foot the while,
And when she saw the little sufferer die,
Bowed her meek head and wept in agony,
  Fancies she hears, in yonder starry isle,
  Her little cherub's voice, and sees his angel smile.

Oh, ye departed spirits of my sires,
And ye, the loved ones of my childhood's days,
While now I look on yonder heavenly fires,
Methinks I hear you tune your seraph lyres,
Methinks I see you bend your pitying gaze
On him who still must tread alone earth's gloomy maze!

Thou angel spirit, who so oft didst sing
My infant cares to sleep upon thy breast,
Let me but hear the rustling of thy wing,
Around thy child its guardian influence fling!
Oh, come thou from the island of the blest,
And bear my weary soul up to thy sainted rest!

Can we forget departed friends? Ah, no!
Within our hearts their memory buried lies;
The thought that where they are, we too shall go,
Will cast a light o'er darkest scenes of wo;
For to their own blest dwellings in the skies,
The souls whom CHRIST sets free exultingly shall rise.

XII.

There is a singular thought in Southey's Ode on the portrait of Bishop Heber. He suggests that many of Heber's admirers—

Will gaze
Upon his effigy
With reverential love,
Till they shall grow familiar with its lines,
And know him when they see his face in heaven!

Why may there not be truth in this beautiful thought? We subjoin an incident which confirms it—an incident which is by far too touching to be false.

"A little girl, in a family of my acquaintance, a lovely and precious child, lost her mother at an age too early to fix the loved features in her remembrance. She was beautiful; and as the bud of her heart unfolded, it seemed as if won by that mother's prayers to turn instinctively heavenward. The sweet, conscientious, and prayer-loving child, was the idol of the bereaved family. But she faded away early. She would lie upon the lap of the friend who took a mother's kind care of her, and, winding one wasted arm about her neck, would say, 'Now tell me about my mamma!' And when the oft-told tale had been repeated, she would ask softly, 'Take me into the parlor; I want to see my mamma!' The request was never refused; and the affectionate sick child would lie for hours, gazing on her mother's portrait. But

"Pale and wan she grew, and weakly—
Bearing all her pains so meekly,
That to them she still grew dearer,
As the trial-hour grew nearer.

"That hour came at last, and the weeping neighbours assembled to see the little child die. The dew of death was already on the flower, as its life-sun was going down. The little chest heaved faintly — spasmodically.

"'Do you know me, darling?' sobbed close in her ear, the voice that was dearest; but it awoke no answer. All at once a brightness, as if from the upper world, burst over the child's colourless countenance. The eyelids flashed open, and the lips parted; the wan, curdling hands flew up, in the little one's last impulsive effort, as she looked piercingly into the far above.

"'Mother!' she cried, with surprise and transport in

her tone — and passed with that breath to her mother's bosom.

"Said a distinguished divine, who stood by that bed of joyous death, 'If I had never believed in the ministration of departed ones before, I could not doubt it now.'

"'Peace I leave with you,' said the wisest spirit that ever passed from earth to heaven. Let us be at 'peace' amid the spirit-mysteries and questionings on which his eye soon shed the light of Eternity."

XIII.

Gone — but not lost.

By Mrs. Ellen Stone.

Sweet bud of earth's wilderness, rifled and torn!
Fond eyes have wept o'er thee, fond hearts still will mourn;
The spoiler hath come, with his cold withering breath,
And the loved and the cherished lies silent in death.

He felt not the burden and heat of the day!
He hath passed from this earth, and its sorrows, away,
With the dew of the morning yet fresh on his brow:—
Sweet bud of earth's wilderness, where art thou now?

And oh! do you question, with tremulous breath,
Why the joy of your household lies silent in death?
Do you mourn round the place of your perishing dust?
Look onward and upward with holier trust!

Who cometh to meet him, with light on her brow?
What angel form greets him so tenderly now!
'Tis the pure sainted mother, springs onward to bear
The child of her love from this region of care!

She beareth him on to that realm of repose,
Where no cloud ever gathers, no storm ever blows:
For the Saviour calls home to the mansions above,
This frail trembling floweret in mercy and love.

There shall he for ever, unchanged by decay,
Beside the still waters and green pastures stray;
And there shall ye join him, with earth's ransomed host,
Look onward and upward! "he 's *gone* — but not *lost!*"

SECTION III.

Consolatory Poetry.

The principal vein which the poets follow when they dwell on this subject is in the way of consolation. These sentiments will serve to show what is the burden of the heart in its deepest sorrow when bereaved of friends. It is the hope of blessed and eternal reunion in a better life. To this it instinctively turns as its joyful song in this house of pilgrimage. In the sighings of the poet we see what the heart wants. This is the great stream, ending in the ocean of eternal love, into which all individual tears fall, and are changed from tears of sorrow to tears of joy. Into this stream the poet merges his mysterious soul, whenever he undertakes to speak for us, or to guide and interpret our own feelings to us. Then he feels what we feel, loves what we love, and seeks what we seek.

It is remarkable and significant that with this doctrine the poets generally end their consolatory pieces. They frequently begin with other sources of consolation, but finally slide into this. Thus the whole is crowned with this much-desired union. This shows whither the heart's wishes tend. Here the aching heart rests, and only here. Here is its home, with what it loves — where else? Even when higher sources of consolation are acknowledged, even when Christ is made the substance of heavenly felicity, still here the heart centres when its sorrows flow from bereavement. Not that friends are dearer to it than Christ, but because that which is the immediate cause of sorrow is most prominent. When one is lost to the heart it leaves the ninety-and-nine others which are safe, and goes after the lost one till it is found. In joy, other attractions in heaven are brighter, but in sorrow and fresh bereavement, this. Nor is this wrong, for He who wept with the sisters of Bethany for their brother Lazarus, is merciful even to our infirmities. Martha did not say to Him, Lord, if thou hadst been here, I would not have wept though my brother had died; but she said, "Lord, if thou hadst been here, my brother *had not died.*" Neither does He chide her, and say, I am here, that is enough; but he rather encourages her hope in the direction of her lost brother, upon whom her heart was now set in the intensity of her grief, as a source of comfort: — "Thy brother shall rise again." It is proper, then, that the poets terminate their consolations in this precious faith.

"In times of bereavement, the mind often becomes utterly depressed and bewildered at its inability of expression, and it turns instinctively to the language of another: to 'the deep sad harmonies that haunt the breast of the poet,' who has foreshadowed a portraiture of our own hearts; and we are comforted by the assurance it gives, that *our* state is not peculiar. In oui weakness of grief we are apt to feel as if alone; as if set apart as a mark for the shafts of adversity; but we now learn the fact, that we are only *one* of the great brotherhood of sorrow." The discovery that we have sympathy, and that others weep as well as ourselves, disperses our loneliness, and takes away much of the complaint of our grief.

The poet is a comforter which all love; he comes to us so softly, so silently, so feelingly. In the tender hour of fresh bereavement we instinctively withdraw from others and love to be alone. We hide ourselves from the every-day contact of those who, though they would, cannot feel with us, and measure the full extent and depth of our grief. "We shrink even from the incompetence of those who, from genuine kindliness of heart, obtrude their sympathy upon us. The common-place generalities to which such persons resort, revolt us, as heartless and hackneyed; the human voice, even, assumes a dissonance, when it urges us to forget a grief over which the heart yearns with a devoted tenderness, feeling as if relief were a treason to the beloved object. Few can afford consolation in periods like these — few should attempt it."

At such times we choose our own comforters, and these must have a sacred priestly character — speaking a language removed from the common-place of ordinary life. The poet suits us. He does not only speak gentle and soothing words, but he makes himself the very soul of our grief, speaking rather *in* us than to us. He has felt the same which we now feel, sought the same relief, and now tells us how and where he found it. His words do not flow coldly from his lips and so fall upon our ears, but we feel them at our heart, welling up from the depths of the soul, warm, tender and living. Thus he affords light to the heart in its darkness, and life in its death.

Truly has it been said, "the poet is the interpreter of the human heart — the expounder of its mysteries. An utterance is given to him which is denied to others, even although their feelings may be akin to his own. Through him Truth speaks: and wild or wayward as may seem her revelations, yet it is the common sentiment, the universal emotion, she speaks; she gives the germ of a nobler principle, the incentive to a higher hope. We weep over his words, relieved by a strange sympathy; find through him a voice and utterance for thoughts too deep for expression; and are at once relieved, comforted, and instructed."

I.

Reunion Above.

Leggett.

If yon bright stars, which gem the night,
Be each a blissful dwelling sphere,
Where kindred spirits reunite
Whom death hath torn asunder here,
How sweet it were at once to die,
To leave this blighted orb afar;
Mixt soul and soul to cleave the sky
And soar away from star to star.

But oh! how dark, how drear and lone,
Would seem the brightest world of bliss,
If, wandering through each radiant one,
We failed to find the loved of this!

If there no more the ties shall twine
Which death's cold hand alone could sever,
Ah, then those stars in mockery shine,
More hateful as they shine for ever!

It cannot be — each hope, each fear,
That lights the eye or clouds the brow,
Proclaims there is a happier sphere,
Than this bleak world that holds us now.
There is a voice which sorrow hears,
When heaviest weighs life's galling chain,
'Tis heaven that whispers—"dry your tears,
The pure in heart shall meet again."

II.

"Sorrow not, even as others which have no hope."

By Rev. Charles Wesley.

If death my friend and me divide,
Thou dost not, Lord, my sorrows chide,
  Nor frown my tears to see;
Restrained from passionate excess,
Thou bidst me mourn in calm distress,
  For them that rest in thee.

I feel a strong, immortal hope,
Which bears my mournful spirit up
  Beneath its mountain load;
Redeemed from death, and grief, and pain,
I soon shall find my friend again,
  Within the arms of God.

Pass the few fleeting moments more,
And death the blessing shall restore,
  Which death hath snatched away:
For me, thou wilt the summons send,
And give me back my parted friend,
  In that eternal day!

III.

And what if the death-pang my bosom must rend,
If it mingles my spirit with that of my friend?
I care not how soon they may sever earth's ties,
For though parted on earth we'll be linked in the skies.

IV.

FROM SACRED LYRICS, BY R. HUIE.

Sleep on, my babe! thy little bed
  Is cold, indeed, and narrow;
Yet calmly there shall rest thy head,
And neither mortal pain nor dread
  Shall e'er thy feelings harrow!

Thou may'st no more return to me,
  But there's a time, my dearest,
When I shall lay me down by thee,
And when of all, my babe shall be
  That sleep around, the nearest!

And sound our sleep shall be, my child,
  Were earth's foundation shaken;
Till He, the pure, the undefiled,
Who once, like thee, an infant smiled,
  The dead to life awaken!

Then, if to Him, with faith sincere,
  My babe at death was given,
The kindred tie that bound us here,
Though rent apart with many a tear,
  Shall be renewed in heaven!

V.

There is no doubt danger that some may comfort themselves with the hope of meeting their friends in heaven, who have themselves no sure title to that blessed place! so deceitful is the heart; and so hastily does it seize at pleasant conclusions, without making all right by the way. What a sore and bitter disappointment will that be, when, instead of meeting their friends in heaven, they find themselves excluded from it for ever! Let the truth be deeply impressed upon our hearts, that if we would see our friends in heaven, our first duty is to become CHRISTIANS. No others shall ever enter through the gates into that blissful city. Let the first two lines be pondered by all who love their friends but love not Christ!

Yes — if I have not sacrificed all other claims to thine,
Surrendered with a selfish love, because that thou wert mine,
I still may hope to feel that bliss within my soul revive,
Which never in this yearning heart will languish while I live;
May hear thy unforgotten voice join the archangel's song,
And know my own beloved one, amidst a holy throng,
May see thee, by the light that breaks the shadows of the tomb,
A portion of my happiness in the bright world to come!

VI.

MY BOY!

I know his face is hid
Under the coffin lid;
Closed are his eyes; cold is his forehead fair;
My hand that marble felt,
O'er it in prayer I knelt;
Yet my heart whispers that — he is not there!

Not there?—Where, then, is he?
The form I used to see
Was but the *raiment* that he used to wear.
The grave that now doth press
Upon that cast-off dress,
Is but his wardrobe locked; — *he* is not there!

He lives! — In all the past
He lives; nor, to the last,
Of seeing him again will I despair;
In dreams I see him now,
And on his angel brow,
I see it written, "Thou shalt see me *there!*"

Yes, we all live to God!
FATHER, thy chastening rod
So help us, thine afflicted ones, to bear,
That in the spirit land,
Meeting at thy right hand,
'T will be our heaven to find that — he is *there*

VII.

NOT LOST, BUT GONE BEFORE.

Say, why should friendship grieve for those
Who safe arrive on Canaan's shore?
Released from all their hurtful foes,
They are not lost — but gone before.

How many painful days on earth
Their fainting spirits numbered o'er!
Now they enjoy a heavenly birth;
They are not lost — but gone before.

Dear is the spot where Christians sleep,
And sweet the strain which angels pour;
O why should we in anguish weep?
They are not lost — but gone before.

Secure from every mortal care,
By sin and sorrow vexed no more,
Eternal happiness they share,
Who are not lost — but gone before.

To Zion's peaceful courts above,
In faith triumphant may we soar,
Embracing in the arms of love,
The friends not lost — but gone before.

On Jordan's banks whene'er we come,
And hear the swelling waters roar,
Father, convey us safely home,
To friends not lost — but gone before.

VIII.

Ye who mourn
Whene'er yon vacant cradle, or the robes
That decked the lost one's form, call back a tide
Of alienated joy, can ye not trust
Your treasure to *His* arms, whose changeless care
Passeth a mother's love? Can ye not hope,
When a few hastening years their course have run,
To go to him, though he no more on earth
Returns to you?
And when glad faith doth catch
Some echo of celestial harmonies,
Archangel's praises, with the high response
Of cherubim, and seraphim, oh think —
Think that your babe is there!

IX.

Dreams of Heaven.

Mrs. Hemans.

O, woman! with the soft sad eye
Of spiritual gleam!
Tell me of those bright realms on high,
How doth thy deep heart dream?

By thy sweet mournful voice I know,
  On thy pale brow I see,
That thou hast loved in silent woe,
  Say, what is heaven to *thee?*

"Oh! heaven is where no secret dread
  May haunt Love's meeting hour;
Where from the past no gloom is shed
  O'er the heart's chosen bower;

"Where every severed wreath is bound;
  And none have heard the knell,
That smites the soul in that wild sound—
  Farewell! Beloved, farewell!"

X.

On witnessing the burial of an emigrant's child, in real sympathy with the bereaved, Mrs. Hemans thus beautifully sings—

And to her who bore him,
  Her who long must weep,
Yet shall heaven restore him,
  From his pale sweet sleep!
Those blue eyes of love and peace again
Through her soul will shine, undimmed by pain.

XI.

Weep not for her! There is no cause for wo;
  But rather nerve thy spirit, that it walk
Unshrinking o'er the thorny paths below,
  And from earth's low defilements keep thee back:
So, when a few fleet severing years have flown,
  She'll meet thee at heaven's gate—and lead thee on!
      Weep not for her!

XII.

This beautiful poem is doubly sweet and comforting, as it has been set to excellent music; thus it has found a deeper lodgment in the hearts and associations of many than it could otherwise have done. I have frequently noticed the deep effect it produced when sung at the breaking up of small social circles, among the young. How many upon whose lips it lingered in parting have not met again! Youthful associates, alas! how they scatter! The circles of our early love,—how the gems have dropped away! In different places, and amid various fortunes, bright and sad, the companions of our early life are crowding towards the grave. So pass we away! May we not hope that the reading of this poem here, may beget in the heart of the reader a stronger resolution to strive after the eternal inheritance of the saints — and at the same time draw forth a prayer for those far away? And will it not open afresh a fountain of true consolation to such as are separated from pious friends?

Reunion in Heaven.

When shall we meet again?
  Meet ne'er to sever?
When will peace wreathe her chain
  Round us for ever?
Our hearts will ne'er repose
Safe from each blast that blows
In this dark vale of woes—
  Never — no, Never!

When shall love freely flow,
  Pure as life's river?
When shall sweet friendship glow,
  Changeless for ever?

Where joys celestial thrill,
Where bliss each heart shall fill,
And fears of parting chill—
  Never — no, Never!

Up to that world of light,
  Take us, dear Saviour;
May we all there unite,
  Happy, for ever:
Where kindred spirits dwell,
There may our music swell,
And time our joys dispel—
  Never — no, Never!

Soon shall we meet again—
  Meet ne'er to sever;
Soon will peace wreathe her chain
  Round us for ever:
Our hearts will then repose
Secure from worldly woes:
Our songs of praise shall close—
  Never — no, Never!

XIII.

O! it is sweet to die,—to part from earth,—
And win all heaven for things of idle worth;
Then sure thou wouldst not, though thou couldst awake
The little slumberer, for its mother's sake.
It is when those we love, in death depart,
That earth has slightest hold upon the heart.
Hath not bereavement higher wishes taught,
And purified from earth, thine earth-born thought?
I know it hath. Hope then appears more dear,
And heaven's bright *realms* shine brightest through a tear.
Though it be hard to bid thy heart divide,
And lay the gem of all thy love aside—
Faith tells thee, and it tells thee not in vain,
That thou shalt meet thine infant yet again.

On seraph wings the new-born spirit flies,
To brighter regions and serener skies;
And ere thou art aware the day may be,
When to those skies thy babe shall welcome the

XIV.

My stricken heart to Jesus yields
  Love's deep devotion now,
Adores and blesses — while it bleeds —
  His hand that strikes the blow.
Then fare thee well — a little while —
  Life's troubled dream is past;
And I shall meet with thee, my child,
  In life — in bliss, at last!

These beautiful extracts from the poets show that the spirit of poetry is in love with this doctrine, speaking of it with the most implicit faith, and giving to it all its own sweet tenderness. Now, by way of concluding this chapter, we cannot refrain from introducing another beautiful poem, with the affecting incident which drew it forth, to show how spontaneously the heart sings of this faith from its deep fullness in sudden emergencies of grief. The soothing strains of similar song, under similar circumstances, have been breathed from a thousand hearts, to which printed verse has never given a local habitation, so that it might reach the eyes and hearts of others. The inner world has also its poetry and its music; and the heart often has words, and a song, which the tongue is too slow to utter. Hence there is a great deal of unwritten poetry, and a great deal of music, that remains unsung. Haply in the instance to which we refer, an utterance was given equal to the burden of the heart, and — oh what touching numbers!

To show these lines in their true light and tenderness, as well as in their strong and beautiful bearing on the subject before us, it is necessary to give the circumstances which called them forth.

The author of them is Mrs. Sarah B. Judson, second wife of the excellent and eminent Dr. Judson, a missionary to Burmah. In 1845, in the forty-fifth year of her age, and in the twenty-first year of her missionary life, this excellent lady's health failed. It was seen that if she remained in the field she must soon sink into the grave. "At last a voyage to America was named, as presenting the only prospect of life." It was finally concluded upon that she, with her husband and children, should enter upon this voyage. The thought of it was both pleasant and mournful. "To America! the land of her birth, and the home of many a loved one; where parents, brothers and sisters, still trod the soil, and where her darling, her orphan boy,* might once again be folded to her bosom! Oh, should she visit dear, Christian America, once more? Yet she could not leave those for whom she had toiled and prayed, during twenty years of her exile, without sadness. Had it been right, she would have preferred to die quietly in Burmah, rather than interrupt her husband's labours; and her heart sunk at parting, for years, if not for life, with the most helpless of her babes — the eldest of the three — only four years of

* The son of her former husband, the Rev. George D. Boardman.

age. But duty demanded the sacrifice; and she had been too long obedient to this voice to think of opposition now. They bore her to the ship, while both fair and dusky faces circled round; and long did the sound of those loved, farewell voices, half smothered in grief and choked with tears, dwell upon her ear and heart. Near the Isle of France, hope of final recovery grew so strong, that it became almost certainty; and now a voice from poor, perishing Burmah, seemed calling on the invalid for one more sacrifice. She dared not go back herself, but there seemed no longer a necessity for calling her husband from his missionary labor. He should now return to his lonely home in Burmah, and she, with her children, would pursue a way as lonely toward the "setting sun." It was after this resolution that the following lines, the last words ever traced by her fingers, were pencilled on a scrap of broken paper. Let the reader observe how naturally and how touchingly, under the feeling of uncertainty whether they should ever meet again on earth, her heart dwells on the prospect of a heavenly meeting.

We part on this green islet, Love,
  Thou for the Eastern main,
I, for the setting sun, Love —
  Oh, when to meet again?

My heart is sad for thee, Love,
  For lone thy way will be;
And oft thy tears will fall, Love,
  For thy children and for me.

The music of thy daughter's voice
  Thou 'lt miss for many a year;
And the merry shout of thine elder boys,
  Thou 'lt listen in vain to hear.

When we knelt to see our Henry die,
  And heard his last faint moan,
Each wiped away the other's tears —
  Now, each must weep alone.

My tears fall fast for thee, Love,—
  How can I say farewell?
But go; — thy God be with thee, Love,
  Thy heart's deep grief to quell!

Yet my spirit clings to thine, Love,
  Thy soul remains with me,
And oft we'll hold communion sweet,
  O'er the dark and distant sea.

And who can paint our mutual joy,
  When, all our wanderings o'er,
We both shall clasp our infants three,
  At home on Burmah's shore!

But higher shall our raptures glow,
  On yon celestial plain,
When the loved and parted here below
  Meet, ne'er to part again.

Then gird thine armor on, Love,
  Nor faint thou by the way,
Till Boodh shall fall, and Burmah's sons
  Shall own Messiah's sway.

In all the missionary annals there are few things more affecting than this. A parting took place, but not the one anticipated in these verses. She became suddenly worse, and died on board the ship in the port of the Isle of St. Helena. They parted on that "green islet," but instead of sailing toward the "setting sun," she soared toward

Yon celestial plain,
Where the loved and parted here below
  Meet, ne'er to part again!

The precious remains of so good a life lie buried in that distant isle of the sea — her spirit is in the land of eternal love. Who can believe that the meeting season, of which she prophesied so ardently in this dying hymn, will not be realized? Will she see those no more for whom she "toiled and prayed" in Burmah, for whom she so much desired the restoration of her health, and for whose sake she was so willing to see her husband return to them, leaving her and her children in the midst of the ocean? Will she see no more those "elder boys," and that "orphan boy," and that "daughter," and "Henry," already in heaven? Is she now for ever separated from her husband, to whom she sung almost with her dying breath:

> Yet my spirit clings to thine, Love,
> Thy soul remains with me.

Who can believe it? See! as soon as she is buried in that "beautiful, shady spot," duty calls him to return in haste to his Master's work. He leaves the place sadly, but not without the consolation of that hope of a meeting in heaven which was the swan song of his dying but now sainted wife. "I was obliged," says Dr. Judson, "to hasten on board the ship, and we immediately went to sea. On the following morning no vestige of the island was discernible in the distant horizon. For a few days, in the solitude of my cabin, with my poor children crying around me, I could not help abandoning myself to heart-breaking sorrow. But the promises of the Gospel came to my aid, and faith stretched her view to the bright world of eternal life, and anticipated a happy meeting with those beloved beings whose bodies are mouldering at Amherst and St. Helena."

THE MOTHER AND HER DYING BOY.

BOY.

My mother, my mother, O let me depart!
Your tears and your pleadings are swords to my heart;
I hear gentle voices, that chide my delay;
I see lovely visions that woo me away.
My prison is broken, my trials are o'er!
O mother, my mother, detain me no more!

MOTHER.

And will you then leave us, my brightest, my best?
And will you run nestling no more to my breast?
The summer is coming to sky and to bower;
The tree that you planted will soon be in flower,
You loved the soft season of song and of bloom;
O, shall it return, and find you in the tomb?

BOY.

Yes, mother, I loved in the sunshine to play,
And talk with the birds and the blossoms all day;
But sweeter the songs of the spirits on high,
And brighter the glories round God in the sky:
I see them, I hear them, they pull at my heart,
My mother, my mother, O let me depart.

MOTHER.

O do not desert us! Our hearts will be drear,
Our home will be lonely, when you are not here;
Your brother will sigh 'mid his playthings, and say,
I wonder dear William so long can delay:
That foot like the wild wind, that glance like a star
O what will this world be, when they are afar?

BOY.

This world, dearest mother, O live not for this;
No, press on with me to the fulness of bliss!
And trust me, whatever bright fields I may roam,
My heart will not wander from you and from home.
Believe me still near you on pinions of love;
Expect me to hail you when soaring above.

MOTHER.

Well, go, my beloved! The conflict is o'er;
My pleas are all selfish, I urge them no more;
Why chain your bright spirit down here to the clod,
So thirsting for freedom, so ripe for its God?
Farewell then, farewell, till we meet at the Throne,
Where love fears no parting, and tears are unknown!

BOY.

O glory! O glory! what music! what light!
What wonders break in on my heart, on my sight.
I come, blessed spirits! I hear you from high;
O frail, faithless nature, can this be to die?
So near! what, so near to my Saviour and King?
O help me, ye angels, His glories to sing!

CHAPTER XI.

Objections to the Doctrine of Heavenly Recognition.

I have heard you say,
That we shall see and know our friends in heaven.
If that be true, I shall see my boy again!
For since the birth of Cain, the first male child,
To him that did but yesterday suspire,
There was not such a gracious creature born.
But now will canker sorrow eat my bud,
And chase the native beauty from his cheek,
And he will look as hollow as a ghost;
As dim and meagre as an ague's fit;
And so he 'll die; and, rising so again,
When I shall meet him in the court of heaven,
I shall not know him: therefore, never, never,
Must I behold my pretty Arthur more!

SHAKSPEARE.

THERE are persons who, though they have any amount of positive proof in favour of a subject, nevertheless doubt as long as certain difficulties existing in their minds are not removed. They have proof enough to enable them to believe, were it not for some objections which they are unable to meet with a satisfactory answer. There is a class of persons also, who are, partly constitutionally, and partly from pride, doubters. They take pleasure in being singular, and seem to consider it a mark of superior intelligence to doubt what others believe. They seem to feel no other mission in regard to truth than to cast up objections to it, and throw difficulties in its way. Such persons never fairly and seriously weigh positive evidence in favour of a given subject, but only seek out objections against it; and if they are able to hunt up a certain quantity of objections and difficulties, they feel safe in rejecting it. They can always tell what they do *not* believe, and *why* they do not believe it; but they cannot so well say what they *do* believe, and *why* they believe it. It does not occur to them, that there may be more objections to *their* objections, than they are able to array against the doctrine to which they object. Such persons are not really in search of truth, have no real hunger for it, and will consequently not find it. They are like one who, professing himself in search of ripe and wholesome fruit, should be seen walking round an apple-tree, eager to see how many dry limbs, how many rotten apples, and how much tainted fruit unfit to eat, could be found on it; and if he found a formidable quantity of these, should turn away in disgust, sure that there was no good fruit on the tree.

Many objections may be found always, even against a true doctrine. Nothing is easier than to show that there are difficulties which lie in the way of truth. Let it, however, be remembered, that if any doctrine can be proved to be true by positive evidence, a thousand objections that may be raised against it cannot prove it untrue. It remains true, even if we should not be able to answer the objections; our failing to answer them proves nothing but our own limited knowledge. We must learn, first of all, in our search after truth, that our own ignorance is not its measure. In regard to the doctrine before us, however, we discover no objections which may not be fully answered; and we address ourselves therefore to this task. This will be expected of us by our readers, and we accordingly invite them to follow us patiently.

FIRST OBJECTION.

The great change which will take place in death.

"We shall all be changed." The change which, according to the scriptures, is to take place, especially in our bodies at the transition of death, will, in many respects, be great. It is very natural that this consideration should generate fears that this change will be such as to hinder recognition, and perhaps render it wholly impossible. This is perhaps the first and most natural difficulty that arises in our minds when we ask the question,—shall we know our friends again in heaven? This difficulty should be removed.

A little careful inquiry into this matter will show, that the greatest part of this difficulty is only apparent. A great change may take place, both in the body and spirit, without destroying those marks of identity and those peculiarities of character by which recognition takes place. The change which comes with death will consist, not in adding any thing entirely or essentially new, but only in an unfolding and perfecting of what is already at hand in us. There is a great difference between a small sapling and a full-grown tree; and yet great as the apparent change is, the marks of its identity continue through all the stages of its evolution. In the different stages of human life, through infancy, childhood, youth, manhood, and age, the same being continues, carrying with him his peculiarities, and preserves from one stage to the other those marks by which he is recognized as the same person. There are features which run with marked prominence through all these transitions. Should, however, these marks in themselves prove insufficient to effect a recognition, they may still serve as hints which, by the assistance of mutual recollections, associations, inquiries and replies, shall lead to a complete revival of former acquaintance.

That the change which awaits us is one, not of transformation, but of evolution, is evident from scripture representations of it. The apostle Paul represents the new celestial man as rising out of the old earthly man, as the new grain rises out of the old. The change is not so much in the outward form as in the inward potence which fills out and pervades the form with a new life. The original form will remain while the element of corruption will be changed into that of incorruption. The dishonour, which in various ways, and in various degrees, attaches to our present life, will give way to glory. Weakness will be swallowed up in power. The natural will pass into the spiritual, the mortal into immortality. Now, all these changes are but risings from a lower to a higher life, which, though they involve great. changes, are not in form but in power. They may all take place without radically changing those familiar peculiarities which make recognition possible. As in life a person is changed from a sinner to a saint, while he still retains, to a great extent, the same external features; so, the elements of power, glory and immortality, may be unfolded in us, in our glorification, without producing any more change in the appearance of that side of our being with which we were wont to converse with our friends, than the positive condition of electricity does upon that which it fills with its mysterious fluid.

> "Gently — so have good men taught —
> Gently, and without grief, the old shall glide
> Into the new."

That gracious life into which we are renovated in regeneration, and which is to become complete in heaven, like its divine Author, does not destroy but fulfil. It makes that which exists perfect, and makes that perfection permanent by making it immortal. The transfiguration of Christ upon the mount was no doubt intended, in part, to give the apostles a glimpse of what they might expect when "he should change their vile bodies, that they might be fashioned like unto his glorious body." There the change which took place in their Master was great: "the fashion of his countenance was altered, and his raiment was white and glistening," "and his face did shine as the sun;" yet still they knew Him from the rest amid that "excellent glory," and they "were eye-witnesses of his majesty." His glorious person was still, as to its external marks, what it was before, and could be recognized as his through the veil of holy light which enshrouded it.

May not the same be the case with us in our glorified bodies?

We have still another illustration of the continuation through death and appearance in the resurrection of those marks by which recognition takes place, in the interview of Christ with His disciples after his resurrection from the dead. When the disciples were together at Jerusalem, after He had risen, He appeared to them in His resurrection body. Luke xxiv. 36–44. From this passage we learn that Christ did not only show his disciples that his body was composed of "flesh and bones," showing them His hands and His feet, but, to convince them more fully, while their joy was too great to suffer them to believe such good tidings, He told them to "handle" him, and He eat in their presence "a piece of broiled fish, and of an honey-comb." Here then they had marks, even in His resurrection body, by which they might have known Him at once, which no doubt they would have done, had not their great surprise amazed and confounded them. By a natural process, however, a speedy and joyful recognition is effected. Just let this whole scene be transferred to heaven; and why may not the like take place there as well as here?

True friendship and affection, moreover, are founded not so much upon outward appearances, as upon inward mutual spiritual qualities. These, it is true, manifest themselves and attract our love, through acts and organs of the body, though much obscured, the body in its imperfections interposing media which blunt the exhibition of these qualities, and destroying much of their impressiveness. Who knows but it may be one of the advantages and excellencies of the glorified body, that it will place a more transparent medium between us and those qualities of soul in our friends which have fixed our affections on them, so as actually to facilitate our recognition of those agreeable traits of character in them which induced us to love them at first? It is agreeable, both to reason and intimations of scripture, to believe that our intercourse in heaven will be more immediate and intuitive, and less through media, than on earth. If this be so, there are no doubt in us capacities for intercourse far more refined and intimate, which are not yet unfolded, but of which we will become conscious when once our spiritual powers and affections act in their refined and glorified bodies. "Beloved, it doth not yet appear what we shall be!" The apostles seem to have felt themselves labouring under the constant consciousness of a disadvantage on account of the medium which their "vile body" interposed between them and Christ, which kept them at an aching distance from Him. John, who not only saw Jesus, but lay upon His bosom, and who seemed, as the "beloved disciple," to enjoy more intimate fellowship with Him than any of the rest, did not yet "see Him as He is;" but comforts the saints with the hope that this shall take place "when He shall appear," and "when we shall be like Him." This same obscurity and imperfection, according to Paul, also characterizes the intercourse of saints with saints in this world; for he is speaking of charity—love between man and man—when he says, "For we know in part, and we prophesy in part. But when that which is perfect is come, then that which is in part shall be done away. For now we see through a glass, darkly; but then face to face." What else can this "face to face" mean, but a direct intuitive communion one with another when in our perfect bodies? In a literal sense they had seen each other face to face on earth, but this was only a partial sight, obscured by imperfections of the body; when "that which is in part shall be done away," and when these "vile bodies" shall no more, like a glass, darkly obscure our view, "then shall we know even as also we are known."

Thus the change which awaits us, so far from hindering us in recognizing our friends in heaven, will be the means of vastly facilitating it. The perfection which the scriptures encourage us to hope for in the heavenly world, will be of service to us in the renewal of affectionate communion with those we loved that have gone before, as well as in other respects.

And shall I e'er again thy features trace,
  Beloved friend; thy lineaments review?
  Yes: though the sunken eyes, and livid hue
And lips comprest, have quenched each lively grace,
Death's triumph; still I recognize the face
  Which thine for many a year affection knew;
  And what forbids, that, clothed with life anew,
It still on memory's tablet holds its place?—
Tho' then thy cheek with deathless bloom be sheen,
  And rays of splendor wreath thy sunlike brow,
That change I deem shall sever not between
  Thee and thy former self; nor disallow
That love's tried eyes discern thee through the skreen
  Of glory then, as of corruption now.

BISHOP MANT.

SECOND OBJECTION.

If it were true, it would be more clearly revealed.

It is said by way of objection: If this were a doctrine, true and to be believed, it would have been more directly, clearly, and fully revealed. If true, this doctrine is full of consolation; and it is therefore natural and reasonable, it is said, to think that He, who would not deprive His people of any source of comfort, would have spoken clearly on such an important point.

Let us look at this objection. The fact that this doctrine is not often, and then only incidentally mentioned, is rather a proof in its favour than against it. It shows that the truth of it was taken for granted at the time when it was thus incidentally alluded to — it was not necessary to propound it formally as a doctrine, but merely to allude to it as something already universally believed. All scripture allusions to it are made upon the supposition that it is an acknowledged truth. In this view of the matter an incidental allusion is even stronger than a direct assertion; for while it has all the authority of a direct testimony, it shows at the same time the absence of all disposition or intention to deceive. Thus, if I say, I travelled under the rays of the hot sun, this is the strongest possible proof that it was a clear day, and in the summer.

Moreover, there are many of the most important doctrines of the scripture resting on precisely the same ground as this, in this respect. Such, for instance, are the doctrine of the Holy Trinity, the necessity of making a profession of religion by a connection with the church, the immortality of the soul, infant baptism, female communion, family worship, and other less prominent doctrines or duties, concerning which we have no doubt. Such doctrines existed in the church from the beginning, were carried down its stream in the flow of their own life; they needed no positive statement, for they were established by the same evidence by which the mission of the church was established, and the mission of those who alluded to these doctrines as true. Just so in reference to this doctrine; its existence in the favour of those inspired persons who allude to it as true, is the strongest evidence of its truth. All doctrines of revelation must, in the nature of the case, come short of logical demonstration. They demand faith *in* them as the way to knowledge *of* them. They are to be regarded as facts existing, rather than as doctrines needing proof. It is doubtful whether we can demonstrate our own existence; at least we would make ourselves ridiculous by the attempt. Yet we know the fact of our existence by the actual life of which we are conscious. So, in revelation; we do not ask, can it be demonstrated, but is it a fact?—is it credible? In like manner, with regard to the doctrine before us; we do not ask, is it positively asserted? can it be demonstrated? but has it existed as a fact? is it so alluded to by the lips of inspiration? has it lived as a reigning idea in the thoughts and hearts of men? is it good and desirable, and can it be believed? If all this be true, what weight can this objection have? We answer, just as much as if we should deny that we live, because it is not positively stated, but only alluded to as an existing fact, granted by all.

THIRD OBJECTION.

The heavenly life will be much higher than this.

It has been thought that heavenly recognition cannot take place, because the heavenly life will be so much higher than this, and so far different from it, that all earthly relations, connections and dependencies, must be swallowed up, superseded, or set aside.

To this we reply, that it is scriptural to say, that the future life will not be a destruction of this, but a continuation of it. We will be higher beings, and different beings there, but not *other* beings. All our affections will be vastly elevated, sanctified, increased and perfected, without any violent severing of them from their past life on the earth. Here on earth, when one becomes a Christian, he rises into higher relations and affinities than those in which he stood before; but this does not annihilate his previous being; it only perfects it. He does not, for instance, become unfit for family relations and social life in general by this advancement, but rather the contrary. His new relation to Christ does not supersede and destroy his old relations to his friends and fellow men. His life flows on as before, only in a holier stream. His affections still radiate, but with a serener and heavenlier light. So in heaven; though introduced into higher and holier grades of social life, the soul will still draw after it what it loved in its state of grace on earth, and continue to turn towards it with the sweetest remembrance.

We are also taught to expect in our Father's house of "many mansions" a *variety* of joys. Granting even that the soul is at times caught up into raptures of bliss, so as entirely to forget whether it is in the body or out of it — so as to forget all the affinities that lie upon a lower level; still, there may also be times when intercourse not unlike that of saints on earth may be desirable, profitable, and of holy relish. The joys of the past are passing sweet! A mutual social review with friends of the joys and even sorrows of earth, may fill an hour of heavenly pastime not unworthy of the place. Especially so, as it will have a direct tendency to inspire deeper gratitude, and incite to louder and loftier praise of God's redeeming love. Will not there the weary rest more sweetly as they remember their former weariness? — will not prisoners and servants feel more joyous in their heavenly freedom, as memory still faintly repeats the echo of the oppressor's voice, from the far-off regions of earth and time? On the same principle, we may believe, will the saints in a higher life reap increase of joy from a review and remembrance of the social life of earth, and will find themselves advanced instead of retarded in happiness by a renewal of those ties commenced on earth and now continued in heaven.

FOURTH OBJECTION.

It will introduce partiality into Heaven.

Will it not introduce partiality in heaven? This question indicates an objection which is at first sight somewhat plausible. It can, however, be easily and satisfactory answered. Should we even find it necessary to believe that, in heaven, friends would love friends more than other saints, this could be without any evil effects. For there no feelings of jealousy will exist to take cognizance of it. No one will stop, in the general joy and harmony which will characterize the heavenly intercourse, to measure, with suspicious eye, the affections of other saints, much less desire to attract any to himself to the disparagement of others. Suppose it even to be known there, that kindred and kindred are peculiarly attached, it could not be regarded an evil in heaven. Do Christians here on earth feel jealous of other Christians because they know them to be peculiarly attached to their own kindred? Certainly not. They rather praise them for it, and themselves rejoice in it; and will not heaven be entirely free from all those unworthy feelings which would create difficulty there in the intercourse of saints made perfect in holy love?

Peculiar individual attachments are not uncongenial in a perfect state of society. On the contrary, it is one of the most prominent and delightful features of grace in this life, that it begets and increases general love to all, and particular love to some. The strongest particular attachments that earth has ever beheld, were formed and continued under the power of the Christian life. Will glory divide what grace has united? Will those ties which grace begets and nourishes be unfit to be renewed in the eternal existence of the saints? The holy preferences, then, which this doctrine might seem to introduce into heaven, are rather to be praised than to be blamed. As the moon, in moving round the earth, does not the less move, with all the other planets, round the sun, so the saints in heaven, who cluster, by sweet silent attraction, around the objects of their peculiar attachments, will not thereby fail to move on, with *all saints*, round the Saviour, as the Sun of righteousness, in the general harmony of heaven.

In this life we may act from various motives, all of which may be right ones, though some may be subordinate to others; so in heaven, we may exercise various affections, and if we should even grant that some are less high and excellent than others, they would not thereby be rendered improper. A small light is not darkness, because it is not so large and bright as a larger one. We might as well say that children, in loving one another, must necessarily disparage their parents — or because stars shine they dishonour the moon. In this world saints have their chief enjoyments in direct communion with God, but this does not exclude and make unlawful those thousand little every-day joys which fall to their lot, and make up their incidental and subordinate comforts.

FIFTH OBJECTION.

The love of Christ will occupy us entirely.

It is said that in heaven Jesus and his love will employ our affections so entirely and eternally, that we shall have no time nor desire to know and to be concerned about our friends; and that even a wish to know our friends, and to renew our particular affection for them, would be a disparagement to Christ. Some have expressed themselves with great extravagance on this point. This objection has the recommendation of having a zeal for Christ, but it will hardly be found to be according to knowledge. Such expressions must be placed in the same class with those which speak, with affected zeal, of the pure spirituality of heaven — as not a place, but merely a state; affirming that where Christ is, there is heaven, even if it were on earth or in hell. It is true that with Christ, and with the love of God shed abroad in our hearts, we have heavenly joys, but we are nevertheless not in heaven, unless we are in that *place* which is heaven. Where Christ is now, there is heaven; and it is nowhere else, be our feelings what they may. In like manner, we may say, that to be with Christ, to behòld His glory, and to enjoy His love, is the chief attraction of the heavenly world; but the scriptures nowhere countenance the idea that we shall do nothing there but stand like statues and gaze at Him. Such fancies betray a strange superficial extravagance. While the Lamb is the bright and glorious centre, in whom all the rays of heavenly love meet, He is, at the same time, the Sun which warms, animates and enlivens all the social circles of the saints which surround Him. While the saints love Him in the light and life of that love which He sheds around Him, they also see each other better, and love each other more, in the same blessed light; just as the brightness which makes the natural sun itself so prominent to our view, is the means, at the same time, of enabling us to see and know the objects around us. His presence there, no more destroys the social life and love of heaven, than the sun makes the earth dark.

It might, with the same propriety, be argued that particular attachments among saints on earth were a disparagement to Christ, and hindered our love to Him. This, however, is not the case, but it is the direct contrary; for, as we have already seen in another place, Christ, by his example, encouraged particular friendships — the family of Bethany and "the beloved disciple" shared his peculiar affections. In like manner children that love each other are not thereby hindered, but assisted, in loving their parents. It cannot, therefore, be, that such particular attachments can, in any way, interfere with full, free and entire love to Christ. They do not so interfere in this life, and it cannot be shown that they will in the life to come. Love to Him, and love to the brethren, cannot be disjoined; for the same life of love which joins us to Him, joins us to each other. Where the one exists the other must also be found; and the more we love our friends, whom we have seen, the more will we love Christ, whom we have not seen.

SIXTH OBJECTION.

Christ's answer to the Sadducees.

An objection has been built upon the answer which Christ gave to the Sadducees, when they asked Him whose wife she, who had been the wife of seven, should be in the resurrection. The answer of the Saviour was: "Ye do err, not knowing the scripture, nor the power of God. For in the resurrection they neither marry nor are given in marriage, but are as the angels of God in heaven." Matt. xxii. 29, 30. All that is here asserted is, that in heaven they do not marry — it is by no means either said or intimated that they do not know each other. The Saviour could have met the difficulty which they sought, in this instance, to throw in the way of the doctrine of the resurrection, by simply denying the doctrine of heavenly recognition, and we may suppose that he would have done so were it not true. He could have said to them: your objection amounts to nothing; for there is no knowledge of acquaintances, and no extension of earthly ties beyond the grave — even husbands and wives will have no knowledge of each other there; and hence your question, whose wife shall she be of the seven? has no force by way of objection. He does not, however, resort to this mode of silencing them. He does not say that they shall not know each other, but only that they shall not marry nor be given in marriage. The reason he gives for this is plain and proper — "they are as the angels of God in heaven" — or, as Luke says, "neither can they *die* any more: for they are *equal* to the angels." They are equal to the angels, not in every respect — not, certainly, in being strangers to each other eternally; but they are equally immortal as the angels: "they *die* no more." Because they die no more, they can need no more reparations for losses through death by means of the marriage institution: hence this institution will not continue in heaven. This does not, in the least, intimate that the affections begotten, and the friendships formed in this relation, shall not be renewed and continue in the heavenly social life.*

* It has been made a question, indeed, whether the difference of sex extends to the other world; and it is characteristic of the Hegelian way of thinking in particular, that it allows but little room for any such supposition, having the tendency always to merge the individual in the general, and to make men mere passing exemplifications of humanity. But this view overthrows in the end the doctrine of a future state altogether; since without the distinction of indivi

This passage may be paraphrased thus: "Ye Sadducees who deny that there is a resurrection, and suppose that this instance gives you ground for such denial, do

---

dual nature, as something continued over from the present life, there can be no sense of personal identity, no true resurrection, or other-world consciousness, in any form. It lies in the very conception of our being as we have here described it, that its individual distinctions should reach throughout the whole man in a permanent and enduring way. Personality cannot be evolved at all, except in such union with a particular natural organization, as to have wrought into it, from first to last, the same particularity, as a necessary part of its own constitution. It is one of the great merits of Schleiermacher again, to have perceived and asserted, with proper force, the claims of the individual over against the authority of the universal and absolute, as a permanent element in the constitution of man. The question before us then, according to this view, is already answered. The multiplication of the race will not extend, it is true, over into the other world, and with this must come to an end also the present significance of sexual relation as concerned in that object; our whole present physical state indeed being but the transient process, by which our being is destined to emerge hereafter into a higher order of existence. In that higher state, we are told, they shall neither marry nor be given in marriage, but resemble in this respect the angels of heaven. The family constitution, in its strict sense, though it be the basis of all morality in its process of revelation, belongs only to the present order of things, and will not be continued in the complete kingdom of God. But we may not suppose that the vast and mighty distinction of our nature, out of which this radical constitution now springs, will come to an end in the same way. Entering as it does into the life of the entire person, it cannot be overthrown by the simple elevation of our mortal individuality into the undying sphere of the spirit. On the contrary, it may be expected rather to appear now under its most purely ethical, and for that reason its highest also and richest form. In Christ Jesus there is neither male nor female, as there is also neither Jew nor Greek; not, however, by the full obliteration of all such differences, but only through their free harmonious comprehension in a form of consciousness that is deeper than their opposition, and able

err in regard to the nature of the future life. The reason of your error is ignorance of the scriptural idea of the reason of the matrimonial institution, which is to people the earth, with the final object also of peopling heaven, by the increase of holy families. But there being no more death in heaven, the reason which induced Moses to command that the brother should take her to wife, viz. to "raise up seed unto his brother," does not there exist; consequently the marriage institution will not continue in the resurrection; and hence your objection to the resurrection on this ground has no force.

We have before remarked, that the mere instinctive attachments of kindred and friends are not in their instinctive character eternal, but that they are designed to be sanctified by grace; and that, in cases where this is effected, their union with each other is a higher, an eternal one; not, however, destroying natural instinctive attachments, but perfecting them. In like manner,

---

thus to reconcile them in an organic way. It is on the back ground of such universal unity precisely, that the differences stand out after all in the clearest delineation which their nature admits. There will be races and nationalities and temperaments, strongly marked, in heaven, no doubt, as we find them here in course of sanctification upon the earth. And so there will be, not in the flesh but in the spirit, the difference of sex there too. Humanity made for ever complete in the new creation will comprise in itself still, as the deep groundtone of its universal organic harmony, the two great forms of existence in which it was comprehended at the beginning, when God created man, as we are told, male and female, after his own image. In this view, it involves no extravagance to extend the idea of sex even to the angels themselves, although they neither marry nor are given in marriage. —*Rev. Dr. J. W. Nevin, Mercersburg Review, for Nov.* 1850.

it may justly be supposed, that the affections creating the marriage relation, in the case of the pious, are raised by grace, out of the sphere of flesh and instinct into the sphere of spirit; and thus, although the meaning and intent of this institution in its earthly sense, comes to an end in death, the relation in its mystical and spiritual sense continues, and its affections, beautiful and holy on earth, are made perfect and permanent in heaven.

The probable nature of the relation, and the propriety of it, which those thus united on earth will continue to sustain to each other in heaven, may be farther illustrated to our minds. The relation of parents to their children, for instance, in much which that relation involves, comes to an end and is left behind, by the formation of new families, of which these children now themselves become the heads. The formation of these new relations does not, however, annihilate the filial and parental affections that were begotten in these relations which first existed; the children, though now in another relation to their own children, and this perhaps a relation in some respects more sweet and peculiar, nevertheless still feel themselves bound back to their own parents in undying affection. Having become parents themselves, they do not cease to be children; neither are their new parental feelings inconsistent with their old filial feelings — both dwell in the sweetest peace in the same heart. Mysterious truth, *the parent is still the child!* So, when those united on earth, in the marriage institution, shall have left behind them the lower ties of their earthly relations in death, the substance of those affections connected with these relations now sanctified, may be elevated with them into the higher sphere of eternal life and love; and though, in the resurrection, they marry not, and resume not their old relations in their earthly sense and intent, yet the affections engendered in this relation, and made eternal by being made holy, may continue to incline them toward each other with sacred preference in a higher state of being. We know that those holy affections which are the precious joy of the marriage state in this life, "cease not with the decay of bodily vigor and beauty induced by old age itself, but reach forward still, with a radiant light that grows only more mellow as it is less tinged with the colouring of sense, far down into the vale of years;" why should we suppose it to end suddenly in the grave?

It is unreasonable, unphilosophical, and entirely averse to the general spirit of Christianity, that such a relation—not in form but in spirit, not in its earthly features, but in the affections which it involves—should ever come to an end. Death itself cannot break its bands asunder, nor take its cords from it. Beyond the grave in an endless life alone, can this mystery evolve fully its precious treasures. No shorter history can afford adequate scope for the full perfection of this relation — a relation which is grounded so deep in the elements and constitution of our nature — upon which the very existence of the race depends — which is strengthened by the mutual love of offspring as well as by the holy influences of grace — which covers so large and important a part of our earthly history — which streams its influences with such momentous power into all the other avenues and relations of life —

and which finds its highest perfection in the life of religion, being made the symbol of its deepest mysteries. (Eph. v.) It cannot be believed that the affections begotten by such a relation and included in it, can in all the fulness of their meaning come to an end with the brief glare of a mortal life. To enable us to believe this, we require more than a thousand objections like the one upon which we have made these observations.

CHAPTER XII.

Another Objection to the Doctrine of Heavenly Recognition.

"There shall be no more death, neither sorrow, nor crying; neither shall there be any more pain: for the former things are passed away."—*A Voice from Heaven*, Rev. xxi. 4.

It has been objected, that if we shall be able to know our friends in heaven, we should have to *miss* some who will not be there. This, it has been thought, would introduce pain and distress into heaven; for it cannot be, it is supposed, that even in heaven we should be able to endure without sorrow the absence of our friends — especially the thought that they are in the world of despair.

This objection, no doubt, more than all other considerations, causes persons to doubt the doctrine of future recognition. This difficulty, though perhaps in reality not the greatest, comes nevertheless more than any other home to the bosom of all; and it is by far the most difficult one to answer satisfactorily, because of those instinctive feelings which come in to obscure the judgment; thus hindering the force of argument, and vastly magnifying the difficulty. It is not so much our minds, as our feelings, that give us trouble on this point. We will carefully examine this objection, believing that the observations we shall make will entirely remove any unpleasant doubts that may have been entertained in regard to it. Let it, however, be distinctly borne in mind, that no objection, however formidable it may seem, can of itself prove this, or any other doctrine, untrue.* God is master of all difficulties; and, although we may not be able to see *how* they can be removed, they will nevertheless be removed if God so wills it.

There are different ways in which the difficulty on which this objection rests may reasonably be supposed to be removed. We will present them in order; and though any one consideration may not in itself give full satisfaction, yet all taken together will, we hope, prove entirely conclusive.

I. In death, all ties which are not sanctified, and

* "If casting up objections is a legitimate mode of deciding a question, we may form, and retort, the same objection, with more reason, against those who believe that we shall not know one another in heaven; for we may say, also, that not knowing the persons, we shall not know whether our parents or our friends are there; and this is likely to disturb the quiet and satisfaction of our minds; but to argue in this gross manner, is to confound heaven with the earth. Grief and displeasure can never be admitted in a paradise of joy and perfect happiness. In this glorious condition, our knowledge shall be so clear, our charity so pure, our love to God so fervent, that, as we shall love all things which God shall love, and where his image shall appear, so it shall not be possible for us to love them whom God shall hate, them who shall bear the marks and characters of the devil."

thus made eternal by the life and power of grace, must be dropped and left behind.

There are many ties which are in no sense, and in no degree, gracious. Ties that have not been formed by the life of religion, and which are not sustained and pervaded by it. There are ties, in the formation of which religion has not in the least been recognized, and which have no religious end in view. *All ties between saints and sinners are of this kind.* These must perish in death.

Let it be well remembered that even the ties of kindred are merely and entirely natural and instinctive, unless they are elevated and sanctified by grace. Though higher in degree they are the same in kind as the attachments of instinct in animal life. These warm affections rise entirely out of the bosom of nature, and have nothing moral in them until they are raised out of the sphere of nature into the sphere of grace by religion. Thus the affections of kindred and of friendship, where religion has not brought them under its power, remain entirely instinctive and natural. Take as an example the fond affection of a mother for her babe. "Whence come those bursts of maternal tenderness with which she is wont to caress the much-loved object? Whence those expressions of heartfelt sympathy with which she enters into its pains and innocent pleasures — the promptness with which she administers to its many little wants — the unwearied assiduity with which she watches over it in the hour of sickness, and the bitter sorrow into which she is plunged as soon as death tears it from her fond embrace? It is the impulse of animal nature—the flow and specific direction of a certain class of feelings, which are not to be accounted for on any principle of duty, or on any consideration of general humanity." Are not in this case all religious or moral motives to love suspended by the strong flow of instinct and nature? The heathen mother does the same. The godless mother, dead in trespasses and in sins, does just so. Yea, do not animals caress and fondle their offspring in the same way? Here then is nature, and nothing else. These affections are grounded in nature; but are capable of, and are intended to be, elevated and perfected in grace. These instinctive feelings are to be superseded by the holy life of moral love. If the mother be pious, these affections are already under the power of grace; her affections stoop into instinctive nature, but rise at pleasure into the higher and holy life of grace. Instinct is glorified and made eternal. Natural love becomes moral. When that child grows up to an intelligent age, and becomes pious like its mother, its own instinctive affections will also rise from nature into grace. The life of Christ, the influences of the blessed Spirit, and not mere instinctive nature, will then mediate between them, and be the highest and holiest media of their intercourse with each other. Grace in the heart of each will then rise to a level and flow together, and they will be one in Christ for ever as members of his mystical body. Nature, as it bound them before, will not be destroyed but absorbed and included in grace, and thus made eternal. The ties of kindred remaining, these new moral affections may frequently ebb and merge back into them and become sweetly human. Thus we see the difference between human affections, that are merely human, and human affections which are gracious and eternal, while they remain human still.

Suppose, however, that the child, in the instance just supposed, should ripen in sin as it ripens in years, while its mother is pious. In that case the ties of instinct will still remain, and the mother will still continue to love her child with the same human love, and her love in the sphere of instinctive nature will be reciprocated by her child; but the higher life of grace, which alone can make these ties eternal, is wanting in the child; hence the tie which binds them cannot survive death. Nature and instinct, with all the attachments which rest on them, must perish. When the child dies, the cord of instinct is broken, and there being no basis for eternal affection common to both remaining, *the relation has perished.* The mother may grieve, and even suppose, while in this sphere of earthly imperfection, that she shall grieve in heaven because her child will not be there; but she may be surprised at last, that her instinctive affections, so far as they were merely natural, to which alone the natural affections of her child gave response, are as if they had never existed. She never had any affection for her child *as a Christian;* the relation was of the earth, earthy, and must meet the fate of all earthly things.

The same may be said of the ties of the marriage relation. The marriage cords are designed to be holy, and must be sanctified by the life of grace in order to fulfil their intent. They may be, and ought to be, mystical and holy; and they must be, in order to be eternal. How often, however, are they also merely instinctive; yea, not even that in many cases, but merely prudential and arbitrary, sinking far beneath instinct into the unhallowed regions of natüre, sense and sin! Even a religious basis is not recognized in them, but the whole relation is regarded as only a civil contract—a thing of the state, and not of the church—a thing of man, not of God—a thing of earth, not of heaven. No religious end is acknowledged in it. If the intent of this institution, in the view of such, extend beyond the low consideration of personal propensities, both in a bad and good sense, and contemplate as its object the civil end of peopling the state, yet it never rises to the religious idea of peopling heaven, and of meeting one day in the land of eternal promise, a seed like the stars and the sands for multitude. Can affections having no higher, no purer basis, live for ever? Certainly not. No more than sin itself, for they are imbedded and matured in sin. When, however, these affections in the marriage relation rise from nature and sin into grace, so that this tie has indeed something in it which makes it an appropriate symbol of the union between Christ and His church, and between believers and Christ, (Eph. v.) then, as in the case of the mother and child, they will be united, not in nature merely, but in grace—not in grace alone, but in nature and in grace. Nature will be sanctified in grace, and will finally be glorified and made eternal. Thus the ties and affections which enter into the natural relation of marriage will continue, but only because they live for ever in the life and love of grace. This is a great, a solemn, a beautiful mystery!

Suppose now, that the husband is unregenerate and

the wife is pious; is it not plain that they may be united on earth in the lower life of nature, which is common to both, and even with much warmth of affection, and yet when both are dead, that which was common with both is left behind with nature, and all the affections which rested on it will be as though they had not been? She, the pious wife, never had any communion with him, the unregenerate husband, in the new and higher life of grace; for there was nothing in him that could make response to her feelings in the sphere of religious affections. There never was any union between them in the eternal life of grace; how then can it be renewed and continue in heaven? She may cherish his memory in grief for a wise purpose, while she lives; but when nature, with its instinctive attachments, dies with her, she will not be conscious in heaven of any sense of loss; should she even remember that such a relation once existed, she will have lost all her affinities for it, and feel no more pain from the remembrance of its existence than the saints of heaven can at the remembrance of those sins from which they are now washed in the blood of the Lamb. "Neither shall there be any more pain; for the former things are passed away!"

That there is this essential difference between affections that lie in the sphere of nature and those which lie in the sphere of grace, no one who believes the scripture representations of this matter can for a moment doubt. Indeed so insignificant, according to scripture, are the mere instinctive relations of nature in themselves, that, however lovely they may exhibit themselves in the social life of earth, they are nevertheless perfect vanity. Like beautiful flowers of earth, they are praised by the traveller that hastens by, but they die where they bloomed. The formation of the marriage relation, in cases where it involves this difficulty, is absolutely forbidden. "Only in the Lord," is the apostolic injunction in regard to the formation of this sacred tie. In general, the forming of ties, with unbelievers or unregenerate persons, is called an "unequal yoking together;" and it is asked with most emphatic earnestness: "What fellowship hath righteousness with unrighteousness? and what communion hath light with darkness?" 2 Cor. vi. 14. Truly it is a yoking, not matching. It is a relation, but no fellowship. It is a mere outward conjunction, cold as the moon, which lacks entirely the lovely life and warmth of an inward union — and how can it survive death?

On the contrary, grace forms ties which do not destroy nature, but raise it up to a higher level. While it unites kindred and relatives more closely than ever, it takes into its embraces "all saints," and drops *all sinners*. So far do the ties in grace exceed all others, that when the sacred writers speak of them, they, for the time being, comparatively lose sight of all the earthly relations of kindred. In this sense the words of the Saviour, which some have even been tempted to censure as cold, become warmly and beautifully intelligible. "While He yet talked with the people, behold, His mother and His brethren stood without, desiring to speak with Him. Then one said unto Him, Behold, thy mother and thy brethren stand without, desiring to speak with thee. But He answered and said unto him, Who is my mother? and who are my brethren? And

He stretched forth His hand toward His disciples, and said, Behold my mother and my brethren! For whosoever shall do the will of my Father which is in heaven, the same is my brother, and sister, and mother." Matt. xii. 46–50. The Saviour did not intend by this expression coldly to disown His kindred — for, as we have seen in another place, He not only loved them, but He loved them particularly — but merely to intimate to them that there are ties higher than kindred; and that, while these affections still lived with Him, they lived in a higher sphere than mere instinctive nature: in the sphere of grace, in which He had strong affinities of love for all that did God's will.

Thus, then, we see, that as there is a natural body and also a spiritual body, so there are natural affections and spiritual affections — and natural affections that may become spiritual. Those which rise out of nature will sink back again into nature, unless they are taken up into grace; and those, and those alone, which rise into grace, will live for ever. "As is the earthly, such are they also that are earthly: and as is the heavenly, such are they also that are heavenly. And as we have borne the image of the earthly, we shall also bear the image of the heavenly. Now this I say, brethren, that flesh and blood cannot inherit the kingdom of God." 1 Cor. xv. 48 – 50. Flesh and blood, and the earthly, in this passage, mean mere human nature without the renovation of grace by "the Lord from heaven." All relations and affinities, therefore, in which a renovated saint may have stood to one of "flesh and blood," who bears only "the image of the earthly," will be broken off and left behind in death, and consequently never become a source of pain and trouble in heaven.

This answer of the objection under consideration, we feel sure, would be conclusive to all, were it not for the risings of natural feelings over reason and faith, while we yet know but in part, thus destroying in a great degree the force of the argument. This weakness of faith, and its disposition to flow in the stream of natural instinctive feeling, may more or less trouble us through life, as we are similarly troubled in the same way on other points; and it may be wisely so designed, in order to make us more zealous for the salvation of our friends and kindred; but we are sure that none of these painful yearnings of nature will follow us through the swellings of Jordan into the land of holy love and pure society.

II. If we should even feel that the above mode of answering the objection is not satisfactory, and that these unsanctified instinctive affinities will not perish in death, we may resort to other considerations in order to get clear of any trouble which this difficulty may occasion our thoughts and feelings. We may suppose that God, who is superior to all difficulties, and with whom nothing is impossible, may interpose his power in some way unknown to us, in order to efface from the recollections of the saints all remembrance of any earthly relations which might awaken painful sensations in heaven. "It is surely," says one, "neither irrational nor inconsistent with a becoming sense of human infirmity, to suppose that the recollection of an unwelcome event hereafter can be voluntarily expelled from the mind, or will have no other effect than to increase the gratitude of the redeemed, and enhance the joys of heaven. Standing on the mount of eternal safety, with what unspeakable delight may we conceive them to look down upon the valley of sin and humiliation beneath them! every painful emotion being absorbed in the overflowings of joy and thankfulness to Him who redeemed them by His blood, and conducted them by His providence, to an incorruptible and unfading inheritance. And since the moral perfection to which they will then have attained forbids us to suppose that memory or any other faculty will be applied to a sinful or unworthy purpose, may we not presume that many of those recollections which now find a frequent, and, alas! unwelcome entrance into their minds, to the great detriment of their peace and improvement, will find no place in the associations of eternity?"

It is, moreover, not at all difficult to believe, that even without any miraculous interposition on the part of God, but just in the regular process of things, the remembrance of the lost may gradually fade from our memories. We see traces of this in this life. Those feelings of grief over the death of wicked friends which were so pungent, and almost intolerable at first, have gradually settled down into quiet resignation. Time flows on, and the wound is healed and forgotten. What even remains of this kind of sorrow in the heart in this world of infirmity and imperfection, may entirely disappear in heaven, as the worm drops his grovelling attachments as soon as he rises into the nobler capacity of a light-winged inhabitant of the upper air. "The circumstance of their being removed *out of sight* of their former friends will probably cause their fate to be contemplated with less lively and pungent feelings. Further, the lapse of *time* will probably co-operate with absence, and eventually obliterate the remembrance of them from the memories of the blessed."*

We will venture the remark that it is proved by experience that in this world the cords of affection which bind pious persons to impious relations are gradually weakened, until at length they have scarcely any power except what remains of the force of instinctive feeling, and the mechanical power of habit. Upon the same principle that unreasonable creatures, long yoked together in the same routine of service, feel a kind of necessity of being together, so these, though the cord which binds them to each other is not love and inward union, but mere outward habit. They chime together, not in the free acts of will, but like the wheels and cogs of machinery; and, like it, their working together becomes daily more loose and rickety in their inward attachments. This process of inward alienation will be greatly accelerated by the disorganization which the rupture of death produces; and, as in heaven the saints will have more intolerance to sin than they can possibly have here, what remains at death of this instinctive and habitual affection will be cast back to forgetfulness with a kind of abrupt and holy violence. Or, if even the remembrance of sinful friends should be, for a time, compatible with heavenly felicity, the unpleasantness, (we have no better word,) of such remembrance would gradually lead to entire forgetfulness.

---

* Mant.

We find that in this world events which afford us no pleasure are not revolved in our minds, and thus by degrees fade from our recollection, while such as are pleasant fill their place and become prominent in our memories, though they may not have been so when they transpired. It is upon this principle, and by this process, that many of the sins of a Christian's past life are graciously made to fade back into dim forgetfulness, and finally into entire oblivion. Thus the past life of the saints, so far as it is marked by any thing that is not meet to enter the heavenly world with them, is followed up by the shades of dark annihilation, while before them in a hopeful and cloudless heaven the sweet stars arise as an eternal protest against the darkness of earth, and an ever-recurring promise of brighter and purer realms on high.

III. In this world, the grief of those who lose impenitent relatives by death is much assuaged by a kind of "hope against hope" that they are perhaps after all saved and in happiness. It has been suggested that this sweet and consoling uncertainty may extend into the future life. Heaven is spacious. When we consider the "multitudes which no man can number," which John saw, when he saw heaven opened eighteen hundred years ago — when we add to their number all who have since died in the faith, including all infants, which are more than one-half of the human race — and when we still add to these all who shall yet be saved from the earth, especially in the latter-day glory, when a nation shall be born in a day — how perfectly beyond all comprehension must be the magnitude of the heavenly hosts, and how almost infinite must be those realms of light in which they dwell. Well has the Saviour said, as if to insure accommodations to the countless hosts of the redeemed, "in my Father's house are many mansions." Whether these many mansions are to be viewed as adapted to different degrees of glory and happiness, or merely as places of extensive accommodation for so many children of God, in either case it affords room in some degree to extend the sweet suspense alluded to into the heavenly world. "The lot of some," says bishop Mant, "may be cast in some of these 'mansions', and of others in others; and hence there may be room for imagining that some are in a state of happiness, though they be not brought to the knowledge of their former relations and friends."

May not this thought be the first to enter the mind by way of reconciling it to the absence of some remembered relatives, if so be that some faint remembrance of these instinctive ties should even revive with the future life of the saints. Then gradually, and by a process entirely natural, the onward flow of time and of heavenly joys may obliterate all recollection of them. Memory, in this life, does not retain all that it has known; and may not this feature of memory, which we here regard an imperfection, become a real perfection in heaven, while it drops gradually into forgetfulness all its unpleasant associations.

IV. We have positive and actual evidence that the knowledge of the fate of those that are lost, even where affection for them once was strong, is not incompatible with the full and happy enjoyment of heavenly felicity.

The Saviour, for instance, is perfectly happy in heaven, with a full knowledge of the situation of the lost, and yet He once loved them. Will any one say that His love for them was not once as strong as ours can possibly be for any of our friends? He certainly did for these sinners what none of us would do for our kindred, while they are enemies to us. "He sticketh closer than a brother." Yet on account of their final impenitency his feelings toward them have undergone a change; so that though He once distressed Himself on their account, their situation does not now interfere with His heavenly felicity. Once their condition cost Him tears, but now He weeps no more! May not we expect a similar change to take place in our feelings? Now, nature rebels against that thought, and is far from desiring such a change; yet this is not the first time that God's goodness and grace have done for us far better than our wishes.

The same may be said of the angels in glory. They once loved those angels which are now fallen. They know also their doom and present situation. Who will say that the love for each other which reigned in the holy hearts of angels, before the fall of some, was not as strong and tender as kindred love on earth can possibly be — especially as all earthly affection is tainted more or less by sin. Yet we know that their joys in heaven are not for one moment interrupted by painful thoughts of their lost companions. In like manner also angels in heaven are acquainted with the situation of lost spirits of men — those in whom they were interested, over whose repentance they waited to rejoice; and though they are better acquainted than we can possibly be with the deep woes of the second death, yet they weep not, nor grieve, over their hapless fate. They contemplate the judgments of a righteous God, not with regret and sorrow, but with humility and adoring reverence.

Though we may not feel ourselves able to decide correctly as to the way and manner in which this matter is adjusted, yet seeing that a similar relation between Christ, angels, and the lost, involves no difficulty, we have satisfactory reason to rest calmly in the patience of faith, and not to suffer difficulties which we see have been and can be removed weaken or disturb our faith in the consoling doctrine of heavenly recognition.

V. The last, and perhaps by far the most important consideration we have to offer by way of answering the objection before us, is that in heaven there will be such entire sympathy between us and God, that our wills will fall in entirely and cheerfully with His will. In the language of another: "We shall have no separate desires or inclinations from Him. We shall see that all He does is wisest and best, and deserving of our unqualified approbation. Here we not unfrequently revolt against His appointments, because we bear within us the remains of a corrupt nature; or because we do not fully comprehend His designs; or because in our hearts the affection for God has not that superiority over our affection for the objects of earth which it ought to have. But in heaven, where not only the dominion, but even the existence of depravity, shall be destroyed in our souls — in heaven, where we shall so far comprehend the reason of God's conduct as to perceive that his attributes must be destroyed if he acted otherwise—in heaven, where love to the creature will justly be subordinated to love to the Creator, our wills shall be so absorbed in God's, as to form but one with it; and, of course, no murmur will escape—no pang rend our hearts—for any of his dealings with those whom we loved on earth."*

That such unity of our wills with the divine will can take place, as entirely to change, not only our natural feelings, but even some of those affections which are in other circumstances seemingly pious, is evident from the case of David's praying for the destruction of his enemies. Piety teaches us to pray for our enemies under ordinary circumstances, and forbids a vindictive spirit toward them; and in no way can this conduct of David, which so often comes to light in the Psalms, be reconciled with the Christian spirit, except upon the principle that his soul had risen into such entire union with God, and sympathy with His honour, that he felt that God was injured in his own injuries, and thus the breathing forth of prayer for their destruction was but the going forth of the spirit of God's justice through him. The second table of the law, which says, "love thy neighbour as thyself," was, in the spirit of David, taken up into the first, which commanded him to love God above all. This entitled him, in very deed, to the appellation of "a man after God's own heart."

This same sense of entire union with the will of God, which exhibits itself so complete in the Psalmist, is in a lesser degree begun in all saints on earth, and will

* Kerr.

become perfect with their perfection in heaven. The martyrs have shown it, in hating comparatively their own life and their own bodies, that they might not break unity with the divine will. If our desire to continue in union with the divine will can thus induce us cheerfully to dismiss our own life, will not the same spirit, possessed in a still higher degree in heaven, enable us to dismiss from our affections those of our friends whose flesh and life were not certainly nearer to us than our own, when we know them to be the enemies of God in heart? Alas for us, if we do not meet in us this willingness! In that case we shall never find ourselves in heaven; for, "if any man come to me, and hate not — (how strong is this expression!) — and hate not his father, and mother, and wife, and children, and brethren, and sisters, yea, and his own life also, he cannot be my disciple!" Matt. x. 37. The sense of this passage is strongly and beautifully in place here. The meaning of it evidently is, that we must so love God, and so love what he loves, that if even our attachments to our nearest kindred should interfere with this love, we must withdraw our affections from them. Is this the feeling of him who would sit in heaven and weep for God's enemies, or grieve at the exercise of His justice, even if those enemies are our nearest kindred according to the flesh? This, which, to our earthly sense, seems a hard requirement, becomes not only easy, but even a delight, to those who love God supremely, and "who walk not after the flesh but after the spirit."

There is a fine example of this requirement and its complete fulfilment recorded in Leviticus, x. 1-8. Nadab and Abihu, the two sons of Aaron, sinned in offering strange fire before the Lord, which he commanded not. Fire went out from the Lord and devoured them, so that they died. This was a severe stroke on Aaron, their father; but when Moses told him that this had happened in accordance with God's declared will, that he might be sanctified in all that came nigh to him, and glorified in the eyes of all people, "Aaron held his peace." Moses commanded two of Aaron's *cousins* to carry the young men out of the camp. But what seems most of all severe to the sympathies of flesh and blood, is, that Aaron their father, and his two remaining sons, Eleazar and Ithamar, the brethren of the two dead young men, *were forbidden by Moses to mourn or grieve for their kindred in this their dreadful fate!* "Uncover not your heads, neither rend your clothes, lest ye die, and lest wrath come upon all the people." No, not a tear for the enemies of the Lord, when He judgeth them, even though they be your children and your brethren! — lest ye show that your mind is not with God's mind, your will not as His will. "And they did according to the word of Moses!"

Is this possible on earth, where imperfection, like a dark veil, covers and obscures our complete knowledge of God's wisdom and love — where all our affections are tainted with some corrupting instincts of remaining unsanctified nature; and shall it not much rather be in heaven, where all the reasons of God's dealings with us shall be more fully known—where all our infirmities shall be left behind, and where we shall be "in the light as he is in the light." Surely then nothing will hinder us from falling in fully with all His ways; we shall approve, not only what we *now* see to be right, and what we *now* feel able to approve; but, forgetting all creatures, and filled with the one idea of God, great, wise and good, we shall be able to join heartily in the heavenly exclamation: "Great and marvellous are thy works, Lord God Almighty; just and right are ALL thy ways, thou king of saints."

Fear not, the prospect of the realms of woe
Shall mar thy bliss, or thence sad thoughts arise
To blunt thy sense of heavenly ecstasies.
There, if thy heart with warm devotion glow
Meet for thy place, 't will solace thee to know
No friend of thine, 'mid those keen agonies,
In that dark prison-house of torment lies;
For none is there but is of God the foe,
An alien thus from thee. The ties of blood,
And earth's most sacred bonds, are but a twine
Of gossamer, compared with what is owed
To Him, the Lord of all! On Him recline;
He shall thy heart of every care unload,
He bid thy day with cloudless lustre shine.

MANT

CHAPTER XIII.

The Doctrine of Heavenly Recognition in its Practical Effects.

Our dying friends come o'er us like a cloud
To damp our brainless ardors; and abate
That glare of life, which often blinds the wise.
Our dying friends are pioneers, to smooth
Our rugged path to death, to break those bars
Of terror and abhorrence, nature throws
'Cross our obstructed way; and thus, to make
Welcome as safe, our port from every storm.

YOUNG.

"WHAT good?"—though this is not the most important question to be asked in the investigation of a doctrine, it nevertheless deserves some consideration, in bringing our minds to a conclusion in respect to its merits. If a doctrine have a good practical tendency, it is a presumption in its favor. Error has no such tendency. It is of the earth, earthy. It always tends to lead the mind and heart towards the seen, the material, the temporal. It tends to beget a cold and sceptical indifference towards the future, and the eternal. It does not increase the warmth of our feelings towards realities that lie beyond the reach of sense. Error is necessarily negative, and of course destructive. It leans not on faith, but on sight. Hence it always comes to an end by running out into fruitlessness. The best service it renders to man is when all its effects die out of his heart.

Truth is fruitful in good; and we have the Saviour's own authority for applying to this doctrine, as to all others, the test: "By their fruits ye shall know them." If the fruit is good, the doctrine must be good and true. We have therefore a two-fold object in view, in introducing this concluding chapter, on the practical tendencies of this doctrine; while, on the one hand, it will add another argument in favor of its truth, it will also aid us in making a useful application of it.

We would earnestly ask, what bad influence the belief of this doctrine can have on those who hold to it? We can think of none. We can, however, think of many good influences which it sheds over the heart. This tree yields only good fruit. We can say of it, as the spouse did of Christ, the tree of Life: "I sat under his shadow with great delight, and his fruit was sweet to my taste." As the strongest influences are always most gentle and silent, we can only describe them in their most prominent features, leaving the mind to fill out the more delicate and lovely details of the picture.

I. A warm faith in this doctrine has a tendency to elevate, strengthen, and purify all our earthly affections. In this busy, bustling, and jostling life, where self-interest and worldliness are such prominent factors, there is great danger that friendship and love be regarded as mere matters of earthly convenience. Amid these mercenary influences the higher affections of the soul become gradually carnalized, and are soon valued, like all things of earth, merely for their present use. Even kindred are often cast coldly away, because they are deemed unprofitable in an earthly point of view. After the manner of Ephraim, "lovers are hired," who love while it yields advantage to them, and cease when the pay ceases; or are themselves dismissed when no more needed. Thus there is a strong tendency to hinge the friendships of life upon the low motives of prudence and policy.

Is it not quite natural that such debasing tendencies should appear, where ties of friendship and even of kindred are supposed to end with earth? Of what use can that be, which begins and ends on earth, but to serve earthly purposes? If friendships do not extend beyond the grave, it is difficult to prove that they are any more worthy of being cherished than other interests which contribute only to earthly convenience and profit. How degrading, however, is this to those ties which are so much praised in poetry, music, eloquence and religion! Just as intellect is degraded when it is not animated by a life and light from heaven, so friendship, when confined to this life, is but as a crazed wanderer, who for our attention returns us only an idiot's meaningless gaze.

How elevating to our affections, on the other hand, is the thought that friendships are eternal if pure; that the ties we form on earth, on virtuous and holy principles, will continue through death, and be made perfect and permanent in heaven! This makes the cultivation of friendship a high aim. Even the pursuit of knowledge, so far as it has merely this world in view, and is unsanctified by religion, is low compared with this; for "charity never faileth: but whether there be prophecies, they shall fail; whether there be tongues, they shall cease; whether there be knowledge, it shall vanish away." All our intercourse with our friends will be more holy and heavenly, if we regard them as those who shall be ours in heaven as well as upon earth. "The addition of a good friend or relative will be the addition of one who will share with us the joys of immortality; who will enter with us into the city of the living God, and be our everlasting companion in glory."

The sentiment uttered by the pious Baxter, in relation to this subject, commends itself as true, to all who are truly pious, and who cannot be content to love what must remain on earth and die. "I must confess, as the experience of my own soul, that the expectation of loving my friends in heaven principally kindles my love to them on earth. If I thought that I should never know them, and consequently never love them after this life is ended, I should in reason number them with temporal things, and love them as such. But I now delight to converse with my pious friends, in a firm persuasion that I shall converse with them for ever; and I take comfort in those of them that are dead or absent, as believing I shall shortly meet them in heaven, and love them with a heavenly love that shall there be perfected."

II. Not only will the belief in eternal friendship elevate and refine our social affections, and cause us to love our friends more tenderly and more holily, but it will induce us also to see the importance of forming only pious friendships. There is a strange recklessness in this respect prevailing. Not only are many of the common friendships of life formed without any reference to religion, but even marriage — if such 'unequal yokings' can be called marriages — are often formed between children of Christ and children of Belial! Such connections would not be formed as they are, were there a deep heartfelt belief that true love and friendship are eternal. There is evidently in such cases no serious reflection as to the final fate of these ties in death.

On this point nothing can be said more appropriate than the following sentiments of Dr. Price. "How shocking must it be to believe that our dearest intimate is one whom we cannot expect to see hereafter in bliss, one who wants the love of God, and who is hastening fast to eternal punishment? How can any one think of having in his bosom an enemy to the order of the world, and a child of perdition and ruin? With what pain must an attentive person look upon such a friend, and what concern must he feel for him? On this account, were irreligious friends to allow themselves time enough for reflection, they would necessarily be the causes of the greatest trouble to one another. Did they duly attend to their own circumstances, the danger they are in, the precariousness of life, and the nearness of the time when they shall be separated, never again to meet, except in that world where joy is never known, and hope never comes; did they, I say, properly attend to these things, they would surely be incapable of bearing one another: their love would be turned into anguish, and their friendship into horror!"

Where, however, the belief in eternal ties is active, no such unholy fellowships will be formed. There will be a holy shudder at the very idea of living in marriage, through life, with "a vessel of wrath, fitted for destruction;" with not only the danger of being corrupted by a relation so intimate and so evil, but with the sure prospect also that ties which now make "a fair show in the flesh" of being love, will end at death in an eternal blank!

Thus a firm and devout faith in this doctrine would not only greatly change our notions of the value of friends, but also of the nature of friendship. The light of love would then have to be the light of piety; and all other dazzling qualities would be regarded but as the false light of a splendid cheat! Love toward others would then be regarded by us — what it really is — the love of God in us; and no ties would be either formed or valued except such as have the prospect of extending into an endless life, to be renewed and perfected in the joyous and holy communion of the saints in light.

III. The belief in heavenly recognition has also a tendency to bring us more strongly and sweetly under the power of heavenly realities and attractions.

We think of heaven but vaguely unless we think of it as the abode of sainted friends. Though our Saviour is the chief attraction of the place, yet He, as the light of the upper temple, reveals to us also the saints as the happy worshippers; thus presenting to our minds these subordinate attractions, begetting in us a kind of familiar home-feeling, and giving to heavenly joys a definiteness which they would not otherwise have. When we hear of a distant country, especially if we hear much in praise of it, we think and speak of it, it is true, yet not in the same way as we do when once some of our dearest friends have gone to dwell there; then our thoughts and feelings assume a definiteness in reference to it, which they had not before. So in regard to heaven, when once we regard it as the home of our sainted friends. Then it is, to us, no more heaven in a vague and general idea, but it is heaven as the abode of our departed friends — it is heaven as the place where we expect soon to rejoin them; — this gives distinctness and intensity to all our thoughts of it. Then our hearts transfer themselves to it, and live in it. Then, in faith,

> Our dying friends come o'er us like a cloud
> To damp our brainless ardors; and abate
> That glare of life, which often blinds the wise.

Much is gained as help to devout reverence and tender piety in thus drawing around us the solemn mysteries of eternity; especially so, if we can recognize by faith the alluring smiles of friends, looking out upon us through the cloudy veil which partly hides its mysteries, like the golden light through the vista of clouds which hang along the evening sky. The love which we bear towards the saints in the triumphant church, draws us towards them with humble reverence. It is a sweet attraction, which causes us to linger, in affectionate longings, on the confines of the shadowy spirit-land. It gives us an indescribable desire for their "silent company." It is said that the home-sickness of the Swiss soldiers in foreign lands was often so strong that they must return to their beloved home in the Alps or die; all was dreary and tasteless to them in absence, while the "sweet home" of their childhood hovered in smiles around them in visions of the day, and in dreams of the night. So it is with those to whom heaven is a Fatherland—the bright home-like abode of kindred and friends. It brings with it an unquenchable desire to leave this foreign land and return home. It familiarizes us with death as a narrow crossing. It keeps the power of eternal things near us; and, to a great extent, converts the valley of the shadow of death into gardens of the Lord, through which lies the Father's pleasant highway, by which His children return to Him and to each other.

We very much need influences like these to break in upon the lower attachments of life, which are too prone to detain our thoughts and feelings. Even when we very well know, in theory, what value to set upon earthly things, we need also to learn the value of heavenly things, in order to enable us to feel practically the vanity of earth. The Poet has truly said,

> 'Tis, by comparison, an easy task
> Earth to despise; but, to commune with heaven—
> 'Tis not so easy.

As already suggested, it is true that Christ, and the things which He has prepared for us, ought to be to us the chief attraction of heaven, and we shall no doubt find it to be so when we get there; but while we are in this world of imperfections, God graciously stoops to our infirmities, and draws us also by the love of our beloved friends as with the "cords of a man." "The memory of the sainted dead hovers, a blessed and purifying influence, over the hearts of men. At the grave of the good, so far from losing heart, the spiritually-minded find new strength. They weep, but as they weep, they look down into the sepulchre, and behold angels sitting, and the dead come nearer, and are united to them by a fellowship more intimate than that of blood."

How soul-subduing is the thought, that but a thin veil, which a moment may lift, divides us from the conscious fellowship of our beloved dead! How solemn the thought that, being raised into a higher sphere, they may even now know much more of us than we do of them. How like devotion does the place become to us, when we sit alone and summon around us their familiar faces; or, when we think of them in their white robes, with harps and palms, bending before the throne or walking in "heavenly pastime." It makes us feel almost like the Publican, who stood afar off, casting a wishful and reverent look towards the holiest place, but conscious of his unworthiness to enter it. A sweet penitence comes over our hearts, and we look immediately to Jesus for a fresh application of his cleansing blood, that we may be made more like those into whose holy society we expect soon to be introduced. When the spirit of earthliness and sense hangs too heavily upon our affections and thoughts, so that we cannot rise to the contemplation of heavenly attractions as we desire, the prayer of the Poet is excusable.

> Ye holy dead, now come around,
> In season more profound;
> And through the barriers of our sense
> Shed round your calming influence;
> In silence come and solitude,
> With thoughts that o'er the mourner brood.

IV. The belief in heavenly recognition presents a strong and touching motive to piety.

How can we, who have sainted friends, continue to live in an unregenerate and sinful state? We have heard of one, who declared that nothing troubled him more in his sinful state than the thought of his mother in heaven! He feared that she knew of it; and he also dreaded an eternal separation from her! Do we believe that our separation from our friends will be an eternal one, unless we repent and become pious? Can we be content one moment longer in sin, when we firmly believe that, should we die in our present condition, the look which we cast upon the face of our dear friend before the coffin-lid was closed, was the last look for ever! — that those eyes, that countenance, shall beam on us no more! — that where he is we can never come! Who can endure this searching thought, and continue to sin on earth while his bosom friend is singing in heaven? Alas! that such infatuation should be found on earth! yet there are many who have parents, brothers, sisters, husbands, wives, and children in heaven, whom they will never see! But is not this in spite of this touching motive to piety? Is it not a strange madness?

Who would not strive to win a heaven
Where all we love shall live again ?

God graciously designs that the death of our friends, and our desire to meet them again, should lead us to piety. "No one dieth to himself." Their death, as well as their life, is in this way to be of real service to us. It is most beautifully said — who can read it without tenderness ? —

Smitten friends
Are angels sent on errands full of love ;
For us they languish, and for us they die.
And shall they languish, shall they die in vain ?
Ungrateful shall we grieve their hovering shades,
Which wait the revolution in our hearts ?
Shall we disdain their silent soft address ;
Their posthumous advice, and pious prayer ;
Senseless as herds which graze their hallowed graves,
Tread under foot their agonies and groans,
Frustrate their anguish, and destroy their deaths ?

In many cases this sweet motive to piety has led to blessed results—no doubt much oftener than is known. "Several years ago," says a Pastor, "I was called to attend the funeral of a child *five* years of age. She had sickened and died suddenly. The father I knew not, except that he was an infidel. This child had attended my Sabbath-school, and she had left behind some interesting conversation with several members of the church. This, after the child had died, was communicated to the bereaved mother for her consolation. At the funeral the mother appeared more deeply interested in the subject of her own salvation than that of the loss of her child. The next Sabbath this family were at my church, and requested prayers that their afflictions might be sanctified. They continued to attend my church Sabbath after Sabbath, and on the fifth Sabbath the father became hopefully pious. Soon after this his wife became pious, and then a sister, and then a young lady residing in the family; and the father, mother, sister, and young lady, all, on the same Sabbath, made a public profession of their faith in the Lord Jesus Christ. That father is now a pillar in the church. This great change in that family was produced instrumentally by the death of that child!" Following their sainted child into a holy world, they felt that they were not prepared to meet it there, and this led to deep and saving penitence. Thus,

> Heaven gives us friends to bless the present scene,
> Resumes them to prepare us for the next.

There are none on earth so near to us as our children. Yet there are no bereavements that occur more frequently than these. Half the human race die in infancy — all grave-yards have more small graves than large ones. There are few parents, therefore, that have not wept at little graves — few that have not infants in heaven! How tenderly they plead, that, since they cannot return to us, we should prepare to come to them. Reader, have you a little white-robed warbler in the celestial choir? Are you content to see his face no more for ever? If you die in your present unregenerate state, where your child is you can never come!

> Those holy gates for ever bar
> Pollution, sin and shame;
> And none will ever enter there,
> But followers of the Lamb.

Far from that blessed abode of innocence and love lies that gloomy land where dwell all the enemies of God. Between you and your child "there is a great gulf fixed." The stroke of death which has separated you, has separated you for ever, except you become pious. Ought not the belief in future recognition press you, in the tender hour of bereavement and sorrow, to decide at once for Christ and heaven — and for an eternal reunion with your sainted child? There are your treasures, there let your heart be also. What you do, do quickly — eternity is drawing nigh!

V. The doctrine of heavenly recognition is very consoling to the pious under bereavement.

How often has it been whispered into the ear of grief! The thought that the separation made by death between us and our friends is for ever, adds the sting of despair to the wound of affliction; but the hope of reunion after life's remaining ills are past, is like healing oil to the wounded heart. Our faith follows them within the veil, and sees them blest. Instead of a sad thought, it is rather a pleasant one. For,

> 'T is sweet, as year by year we lose
> Friends out of sight, in faith to muse,
> How grows in Paradise our store.

"Is not the bitterness of their death thus removed, and its sting extracted? Can we not with Job say, 'The Lord gave, and the Lord hath taken away; blessed be the name of the Lord?' Can we not with Aaron exclaim, 'It is the Lord, let him do as seemeth to him good?' Can we not with David rejoicingly declare,

'They cannot come to us, but we can go to them?' Yes, we can go to them. 'They are not lost, but gone before.' There, in that world of light, and love, and joy, they await our coming. There do they beckon us to ascend. There do they stand ready to welcome us. There may we meet them, when a few more suns or seasons shall have cast their departing shadows upon our silent grave. Then shall our joy be full and our sorrows ended, and all tears wiped from our eyes."*

What greater consolation can such have, who have departed children, than to be able to say in the full assurance of faith: "I know that my Redeemer liveth;" and then, looking heavenward, add the Saviour's words in reference to their children: "Of such is the kingdom of heaven!" "We have known," says a Moravian missionary in Labrador — "We have known what it is to mourn over the loss of beloved children, having accompanied two to their resting-place during our service in this distant land. I was once standing by the grave of my departed children, under a brilliant sun and cloudless sky, when suddenly a light shadow passed over the green turf. Looking up for the cause, I beheld a snow-white gull winging her lofty flight through the air. The thought immediately struck me — thus it is with the dear objects of my mournful remembrance. Here indeed lies the shadow, but above is the living principle. Nor was the reflection without comfort to my wounded spirit, since of such is the kingdom of heaven."

The thought that many of our friends have gone be

---

* Smyth.

fore us, and that we shall shortly rejoin them in heaven, must be peculiarly animating and consoling to us, at that trying hour when we ourselves shall be called to die. Death will be but going away from friends on earth to join a greater number in heaven; and, in addition to this, we have also the assurance that even those we leave behind will soon follow us. Death, in that case, will be like going home. It will be but a short farewell to those we leave behind, and an eternal reunion with those who have gone before. Dying will be as when one taketh rest in sleep — and oh! what a blissful waking!

The same reasons which induce us to believe in a final reunion with our sainted friends, encourage and warrant us also in the belief that they now remember us and feel interested in us. This idea too is full of consolation! It is sweet to be remembered by friends on earth, but how much more so to be assured that we live in the memory of those who are now saints in light. Being raised higher, their interest in us must increase in proportion as they become acquainted with those heavenly joys which await us also, and which they already possess. As they approach towards their perfection, their benevolence and love must increase; and, when we consider that we think most about our friends when we ourselves are most blest, we cannot but believe that they regard us with special concern. To have friends in heaven, then, is to have an inheritance in which we may well delight, and after which we are sweetly constrained to long. We, who are heirs of such celestial treasures, may enter fully into the spirit of the Poet's holy boasting —

My boast is not, that I deduce my birth
From loins enthroned, and rulers of the earth;
But higher far my proud pretensions rise—
The son of parents passed into the skies!

Adieu, reader — this is the end! A kind of lovely loneliness gathers around me, as I am about to lay down my pen. Withdraw not your mysterious presence from me, ye sainted watchers! Ye have been an host around me, that came at the call of faith, in those loveliest hours of my life, while engaged in setting down the thoughts of this book. Look still on me through the veil, and let me still feel the calming influence of your blessed communion. Leave me not alone! The earth is gloomy and sad from the curse. It shines but as a cold moon, with a borrowed light. My soul is weary of these storm-swept solitudes outside of holy Eden. Hail! ye far-off lands of light. Hail! ye happy dwellers in the peaceful Salem of purity and love! "Oh that I had wings like a dove! for then would I fly away, and be at rest."

What remains eternity will reveal!

THE END.

www.ingramcontent.com/pod-product-compliance
Lightning Source LLC
LaVergne TN
LVHW010221110826
845151LV00004B/1172

* 9 7 8 1 4 2 5 5 2 6 4 6 7 *